2 to 22 D[...]
IN THE
PACIFIC NORTHWEST

THE ITINERARY PLANNER

RICHARD HARRIS

John Muir Publications
Santa Fe, New Mexico

Originally published as *22 Days in the Pacific Northwest*

Other JMP titles by Richard Harris
2 to 22 Days in the American Southwest
2 to 22 Days in Florida
2 to 22 Days in Texas
Unique California

This book is dedicated to my parents, Carl and Ruth Harris of Lynnwood, Washington, who made it possible.

This eighteenth volume in the 2 to 22 Days series is a special labor of love. It brings the series full circle to Edmonds, Washington, where it originated. Special thanks to the following people for their suggestions and encouragement: Rick Steves; Gene Openshaw; Carl Franz and Lorena Havens; Terry and Brett Harris; Lee, Terri, Christopher, and Shannon Harris; Kent Williamson; and, most of all, Rita Guidi, whose artistic inspiration and environmental awareness let me see Washington and Oregon as if for the first time.

John Muir Publications, P.O. Box 613, Santa Fe, NM 87504
©1988, 1991, 1992, 1993, 1994, 1995 by Black Mesa
  Productions, Inc.
Cover and maps ©1988, 1991, 1992, 1993, 1994, 1995 by John
  Muir Publications
All rights reserved.
Printed in the United States of America
First printing March 1995

ISSN 1059-2954
ISBN 1-56261-207-7

Cover photo Leo de Wys, Inc./J. Ratti
Design Mary Shapiro
Maps Holly Wood
Typesetting Sarah Johansson
Printer Banta Company

Distributed to the book trade by
Publishers Group West
Emeryville, California

CONTENTS

2 to 22 Days in the Pacific Northwest

HOW TO USE THIS BOOK

2 to 22 Days in the Pacific Northwest takes you on a journey of discovery around a unique, diverse corner of the United States. Along the way, you'll wander through wildflower meadows on the slopes of a towering volcano, its fiery soul shrouded in perpetual ice. You'll venture into uninhabited desert where rainbow-hued sands conceal the bones of prehistoric camels and saber-toothed cats. You'll reach out and touch strange living creatures in lava tide pools along sea-swept headlands and, just minutes away, stroll for miles along soft beaches where yours may be the only footprints.

You'll find an exquisite art museum in a French-style château far from civilization, hike through wild woodlands right in the heart of a big city, and sit quietly in an Indian longhouse as ghostly murmurs in an ancient tongue transport you to the dim past. Wildlife, too, abounds in the Pacific Northwest, and you may encounter rare opportunities to watch a bald eagle soaring free, photograph a buffalo or a mountain goat, or glimpse a killer whale.

These are just a few of the memorable experiences that await as you follow the suggestions in this guidebook. *2 to 22 Days in the Pacific Northwest* contains a tested mile-by-mile travel itinerary for a three-week trip that will take you to the most fascinating places in Washington and Oregon as well as the major cities of British Columbia. The tour, which begins and ends in Seattle, follows a 2,500-mile meandering loop, mostly on less-used secondary highways. It takes you up the Pacific Coast from the California state line to the Canadian border, across the Cascade Mountains and the Columbia River four times each, and through central Washington's apple orchards and eastern Oregon's volcanic desert.

If you have less than three weeks to explore, this tour divides easily into segments for several weekend and three-day excursions out of Seattle, as well as separate full-week explorations of Washington and Oregon.

If you have more than three weeks, you'll find a wide selection of places that invite you to linger, as well as itinerary options that can expand your trip to a month or more. This tour route also connects with John Muir Publications' *2 to 22 Days in California* by Roger Rapoport.

The itinerary format is divided into 22 daily sections, containing:

1. A **suggested schedule** for each day's travel and sightseeing.

2. A detailed **travel route** description for each driving and boat travel segment of your trip.

3. **Sightseeing highlights**, rated in order of importance: ▲▲▲ Don't miss, ▲▲ Try hard to see, and ▲ See if you get a chance.

4. A suggested **campground** for each night of the trip, as well as **lodging** and **restaurant** recommendations for those who choose not to camp.

5. **Helpful hints** and **insights**—random tidbits that will enhance your trip.

6. **Itinerary options**—excursion suggestions for travelers who have extra time.

7. User-friendly **maps** designed to show you what the road ahead is really like.

Planning Your Itinerary

Variety is the spice of any pleasure trip, and nowhere in the world will you find more vivid contrasts than in the Pacific Northwest. This trip contains more than its share of sudden transitions. You can start your day on the shore of a small misty island, return to the mainland, and drive to the crest of a rugged mountain range in time for lunch. You can wake in a big city, then travel through luxuriant forests, and find yourself in a vast uninhabited desert the same afternoon.

The itinerary set forth in this book is essentially my personal dream vacation. To make it yours, study each day with pencil in hand, circling what appeals to you most, crossing out what doesn't suit your style, making notes in the margins. Customize it. If your travel plans include visiting a maiden aunt in Salem or an old army buddy in Puyallup, or going out of your way to see the Bing Crosby Museum in the crooner's hometown, Spokane, feel free to bend this itinerary to suit your own needs and interests. I've included more sightseeing highlights in this book than you're likely to want to visit if you enjoy traveling at a relaxed pace, leaving you the freedom to be spontaneous.

To get the most out of touring the Pacific Northwest, it is essential that you have an itinerary—a realistic day-by-day travel plan—and stick to it. Especially during the summer months, reservations must be made weeks or even months in advance at some places, such as national park inns, many of the best coastal campgrounds, and the Ashland Shakespeare Festival. Without reservations, you'd miss out on some of the best experiences to be found in the region. Once you've made them, they're difficult to change. A well-planned itinerary helps you make sure you won't have to. The purpose of this 2 to 22 Days itinerary is to make trip planning easy, so you don't miss out on any of the best that the Northwest has to offer.

I sincerely hope that you enjoy your northwestern trip as much as I've enjoyed gathering this information to share with you.

When to Go
July and August offer the most consistently beautiful weather in the coastal and mountain areas of the Pacific Northwest. Because the fair weather season is short, travel during these months also means heavy tourist crowds and rigid reservation requirements.

I'd opt for September, the late summer "shoulder season" beginning right after Labor Day. The weather is still fine everywhere, all sightseeing highlights remain open, family tourism magically thins out as school starts, traffic lightens, lodging rates drop, and reservations requirements are forgotten. Wait a few more weeks (or rearrange this itinerary to put Days 9 through 11 toward the end) and you can catch central Washington's apple harvest/Oktoberfest season.

Late May to early June is also a good time to travel. Flowers, both wild and domestic, are everywhere at that time of year. The only drawback is that some mountain areas—notably the road around Crater Lake—are still snowbound.

As for spring . . . I've taken this trip in April, camping all the way in an unheated mini motor home without suffering uncomfortable cold, and enjoyed it immensely. Several mountain areas still had enough snow to ski on, however, and the North Cascades Highway (Day 8), the Stevens Canyon/Cayuse Pass Road on Mount Rainier (Day 10), the forest roads around Mount St. Helens (Day 11), the Cascade Lakes Highway (Day 15), and the Crater Lake Rim Drive (Day 16) had not opened for the season yet.

If you're visiting the Pacific Northwest between mid-October and March, 80 percent of this itinerary does not apply. Photocopy the pertinent pages, then put the book aside for another time, or give it to someone you love for Christmas. Your ideal winter itinerary should be built around storm watching (the latest tongue-in-cheek spectator sport on the Oregon coast) and the world's finest cross-country skiing.

Camping

Camping allows you maximum flexibility in a tour of the Pacific Northwest. While lodging is available in most areas covered by this itinerary, camping facilities offer a more pleasant environment, usually surrounded by trees and near a lake, river, or seashore. The major exception is the greater Seattle area, where campsites are as scarce as hen's teeth, and a hotel is the best bet even for motor home travelers. Camping can also be a problem at busy times on San Juan Island, which has very few public campsites.

Only public campgrounds—state parks, national parks, and national forests—are recommended in this book. Besides these, most places along the route you'll find private campgrounds and RV parks nearby. As a general rule, private parks have less to offer in the way of natural beauty and cost a bit more (typically $12 a night); they can sometimes be appealing, though, for their shower and laundry facilities. Any KOA-affiliated campground can supply information on other KOAs nationwide, and comprehensive, reliable directories covering private campgrounds and RV parks are published annually by Rand McNally and Woodall. Besides ensuring roadside emergency service in case you need it, the American Automobile Association (AAA) publishes very informative campground directories for its members.

Almost anywhere you go in Washington or Oregon, you'll find a state park campground nearby. Both states provide outstanding camping facilities, including water/electric and sewer hookups at most campsites. Most have coin-operated hot showers. Many state parks have separate areas for tent campers. National forest and national park campgrounds usually do not have hookups or showers.

Nightly camping fees at Oregon state parks are $10 (full hookups) or $8 (tent sites) between Memorial Day and Labor Day, $3 less off-season. Washington state parks charge $8.50 (full hookups) or $6 (tent sites) year-round. National forest campgrounds usually charge $7 a night, and national parks usually charge $6 in addition to the park admission fee.

The most popular state park campgrounds in both Washington and Oregon operate on a reservation system between Memorial Day and Labor Day. Campgrounds recommended in this book that require reservations during the summer are: in Washington—Moran State Park (Orcas Island, Day 4), Lake Chelan State Park (Days 8 and 9), and Fort Canby State Park (near the mouth of the Columbia River, Day 19); in Oregon—Honeyman State Park (near Florence, Day 18) and Fort Stevens State Park (near the mouth of the Columbia River, Day 19). Reservations, which can only be made by mail, must be prepaid. You can't get a cash refund if you cancel, though you can change reservation dates contingent on space availability. If you are planning to travel during the summer season, these campground reservations call for careful itinerary planning several weeks in advance. Study the information in Days 6, 8, 9, 18, and 19, and contact the state park system campground hotlines—Washington, (800) 562-0990, within Washington summer only, or (206) 753-2027; Oregon, (800) 452-5687, within Oregon summer only, or (503) 238-7488—to request reservation forms. Campsites that have not been reserved are available on a first-come, first-served basis, but there can be stiff competition for them.

Lodging

For travelers who don't wish to camp—at least, not every night—I've included suggestions for out-of-the-ordinary accommodations almost every night of the trip. (On three nights, in central Washington and John Day Country, even run-of-the-mill motel accommodations are few and far between; I'll simply tell you where to look for them.) Lodging recommendations include bed and breakfasts, historic hotels, unusual resorts, national park inns, elegant small hotels, and youth hostels.

National park inns require itinerary planning far in advance, since reservations are almost essential. If you're lucky, you can sometimes get a room there on short notice due to a cancellation if you inquire at the desk around 4:00 p.m., but don't count on it. These inns, most of them Depression-era historic buildings characterized by rustic grandeur, are located in incomparably beautiful natural settings, yours to enjoy after the crowds of daytime visitors have left. A stay at Paradise Inn on the side of Mount Rainier or the lodge on the rim of Crater Lake is particularly memorable and well worth arranging ahead of time.

Bed and breakfasts (B&Bs) also require reservations, though not as far in advance. Most B&Bs recommended in this book are intimate turn-of-the-century places, with fewer than ten guest rooms, where you can get to know your hosts on a first-name basis. For a comprehensive survey of B&Bs in Washington and Oregon (and elsewhere), consult the current edition of Pamela Lanier's *Complete Guide to Bed & Breakfasts, Inns and Guesthouses in the United States and Canada*, available in fine bookstores.

Hostels, as well as very low cost lodgings that offer private rooms, are mentioned wherever they can be found along this route. Hostels aren't for everybody, but they are inexpensive—$10 or less. They offer clean, attractive, dormitory-type accommodations, usually require an American Youth Hostel (AYH) membership, which you can purchase on the spot for a few dollars, and require that you supply your own bed sheets (or rent them at a small additional fee). Hostels usually close during the middle of the day and observe "lights-out" rules and curfews. If you're willing to put up with these restrictions, hostels provide a roof over your head for about the same price as a campsite. Sometimes called "youth hostels," these places are now popular with budget travelers of all ages, including youthful senior citizens. Hostels attract more than their share of foreign guests and offer the best opportunities to compare impressions of America with European and Asian visitors. If you'd like to meet one or more temporary traveling companions, a hostel is the place to do it: many people who stay there are public transportation travelers eager to share driving expenses for a chance to see places that are only accessible by private vehicle.

I've also recommended a handful of elegant, expensive hotels and resorts along the route, including the finest in Seattle and Portland. These suggestions are not just for the rich. In the matter of lodging, as in all things, variety is the key to maximum vacation pleasure. I recently met a retired couple who travel around America staying in hostels and YMCAs six nights a week and high-priced luxury hotels on the seventh night. Elegance, they told me, is all the more enjoyable when it is a sometime thing, and it costs them less than if they spent every night in a drab budget motel. A luxury hotel can also make for the ultimate "splurge break" from camping. (Hint: If you're wearing camping clothes and a three-day beard stubble, and you walk into a hotel that has a porte cochere, a uniformed doorman, a concierge with an Oxford accent, and marble columns in the two-story lobby, it's extremely helpful to have a credit card and confirmed reservations.)

Food

Restaurant suggestions in this itinerary include places I've personally tried and found exceptional, as well as others that have come highly recommended by local residents whose judgment I trust in matters of cuisine. When possible, I've tried to provide restaurant suggestions in all price ranges, focusing on famous local favorites and less known but equally special eating places. While I have not mentioned national fast-food chain locations or good-but-ordinary "family-style" restaurants, an assortment of each can be found in all fair-sized towns along the route. The restaurants listed are only a selective sampling, and no inference should be drawn about the quality of any dining establishment from the fact that I've omitted it.

The availability and selection of picnic foods in most parts of the Northwest, along with the spectacular array of natural settings in which to enjoy them, mean that you could easily and pleasurably spend three weeks touring the region without ever resorting to restaurant fare. In the Puget Sound area and along the Oregon coast, fresh food is an obsession of many residents, and you'll find farmers' markets, fish markets, and innumerable small shops that sell salmon (fresh and smoked), shark (tastes much better than it sounds, with a texture more like chicken than fish), Dungeness crabs, steamed clams, and a vast assortment of other seafood, as well as some of the healthiest looking farm produce you've ever seen. Besides fish and shellfish, other northwestern food specialties include cranberries, fresh forest mushrooms, cheeses, and wines. The coastal Northwest also has more than its share of bakeries and gourmet food shops, and even the typical shopping mall supermarket west of the Cascades offers variety and quality that will amaze visitors from most inland parts of America.

As you travel to the east side of the Cascades in both Washington and Oregon, the food situation changes radically. In some areas exceptional restaurants are hard to come by, and supermarket shopping offers nothing special. Before heading for the "dry side," stock up on foods that will keep for several days (such as smoked, dried, and canned delicacies) so you can be glad you did instead of sorry you didn't. Central Washington does produce an abundance of the red delicious apples for which the state is famous, as well as pears, cherries, and other fruit, and vendors' stands line the roadsides at harvest time. As you move farther south, you'll also find good buys on farm-fresh vegetables. The Yakima Valley, for example, grows more asparagus than any other place in the world.

Recommended Reading

One of the most vital pieces of supplementary information for this trip, along with the free Washington State Ferries *Sailing Schedules* and *Fares and Tolls* pamphlets (see Day 3), is a tide table. Tides, which rise and fall twice a day by as much as 20 feet, changing the character of the coast-line, are an important factor in deciding where to stop and enjoy coastal areas. Beaches are widest at low tide, and the best time to beachcomb or explore tide pools is just before low tide. For photographers, the ocean crashes against rocky shores most dramatically around high tide. The handiest tide tables are calendars that show high and low tides graphically as curves, but these are hard to find. Pocket-sized tide table books costing about $1 are readily available at boating supply shops and many bookstores. Daily high and low tides are also published in the weather reports of all major newspapers. (Northwesterners assert that this is the only reliable piece of information in the weather forecast.)

The abundance of bird life in the Pacific Northwest is absolutely astonishing. A field guide to western birds (along with a pair of binoculars) will help you appreciate it—and keep children occupied while you drive. I recommend the Peterson guides, with color plates grouped by species to make identification easy for beginning bird-watchers. Nature enthusiasts will also find field guides to wildflowers and marine life useful on this trip.

Hiking suggestions in this itinerary are limited for the most part to trails you can walk in a few hours, barely hinting at the possibilities that exist in northwestern mountains. Serious hikers should visit a Seattle bookstore and pick up one or several of the excellent hiking guides published by The Mountaineers (306 2nd Avenue W, Seattle, WA 98119), such as the Footsore series by Harvey Manning (four volumes) and the Trips and Trails series by E. M. Sterling (three volumes). Marge Mueller's *The San Juan Islands Afoot and Afloat*, also published by The Mountaineers, will tell you what's on all the islands where the ferry doesn't stop.

A thoroughly enjoyable look at Seattle's early history is Underground Tours founder Bill Speidel's *Sons of the Profits (or, There's No Business Like Grow Business: The Seattle Story 1851-1901)*. Another of Mr. Speidel's books, *The Wet Side of the Mountains*, is the most detailed and entertainingly practical guide I've seen to the Puget Sound area. Both are from Nettle Creek Publishing Company, available in virtually all Seattle bookstores or from the Underground Tours ticket office at Doc Maynard's in Pioneer Square.

History buffs may want to brush up on the Lewis and Clark expedition before or during this trip. The explorers' journals are published in low-priced editions by Penguin, Bantam, and Mentor.

If you're planning to explore deeper into Oregon, search hard for Ralph Friedman's self-published *Oregon for the Curious*, a remarkably exhaustive, mile-by-mile, "shunpiking" guide to practically every road in the state. Finally, whether you're traveling with youngsters or just the young at heart, take a look at Rick Steves's *Kidding Around Seattle*, from John Muir Publications. A veteran travel writer from the northern suburbs of Seattle who originated the 22 Days series in 1985, Rick has rediscovered his hometown in the company of his children. The result is this deceptively slender and altogether enchanting book, brimming with fresh insights guaranteed to brighten the drizzliest of vacation days. For ordering information, see the catalog pages in the back of this book.

2 to 22 Days in the Pacific Northwest is a loop trip. You can start anywhere on the circle. Seattle is the most convenient starting point for people coming from the interior of the United States via Interstate 90 (as well as for people who are fortunate enough to live in Seattle). If you are coming up the coast from California, start with Day 18, and, after Day 22, go to Day 1. If you're a Portlander, start at Day 13.

For those with less time to travel, this itinerary breaks up nicely into several shorter trips. Days 1 and 2 contain plenty to keep you busy in the Seattle area. Days 3 through 11 make a great week-long trip from Seattle; Days 20 through 22 also provide a good excursion from Seattle. Similarly, Days 12 through 19 make for a wonderful one-week tour of Oregon.

DAY 1 Begin your tour of downtown Seattle at the waterfront. Visit Pike Place Market, take the Underground Tour in Pioneer Square, see the nation's largest Japanese supermarket, and ride the monorail to the Space Needle.

DAY 2 Explore more of Seattle. Options include urban forest hikes, boat watching at Chittenden Locks, and visits to assorted museums featuring everything from art to airplanes.

DAY 3 Leave the Seattle area: this is the first day of the rest of your trip. On the journey north to Anacortes, the gateway to the San Juan Islands, you'll visit a Salish Indian museum, a New England-style historic town, and the longest island in the United States.

DAY 4 Begin your two-day island-hopping sojourn in the San Juans with a scenic ferry cruise to Orcas Island, where you can spend the afternoon strolling on the lakeshore or climbing the highest mountain in the islands. Camp by a lake or spend the night at your choice of two very different resorts.

DAY 5 Your day on San Juan Island includes a visit to a renowned whaling museum, a whale-watching picnic lunch, and stops at the twin sites of one of the longest—and quietest—"wars" in U.S. history. Later, cross into Canada.

DAY 6 Explore Victoria, the capital of British Columbia, on Vancouver Island. See one of North America's most beautiful formal gardens, elegant British colonial architecture, and totem poles.

DAY 7 Returning to the mainland at Vancouver, British Columbia, you'll have a chance to explore both the old and new sides of downtown, including the city's large Chinese-American community, and visit the world's best Northwest Coast Indian museum.

DAY 8 After crossing the border back into the United States, drive from the seashore to the desert via the North Cascades Highway, through the most spectacular mountain scenery in the United States. Along the way, stop and hike a short portion of the Pacific Crest Trail.

DAY 9 Enjoy an all-day boat cruise up long, narrow Lake Chelan into the heart of the North Cascades.

DAY 10 Drive through Washington's apple orchard country to Leavenworth, the cutest little Bavarian town in the Pacific Northwest's "Alps." Later you'll have a chance to visit the outstanding cultural center of the Yakima Indians. End your day at Paradise on the side of Mount Rainier.

DAY 11 Wander the back roads and trails of Mount St. Helens, exploring the volcanic wasteland. Spend the night on the volcano's south slope, or head to Portland at day's end.

DAY 12 Relax today in Portland. Explore the downtown area's riverside park, historic districts, public art, and unusual architecture.

DAY 13 From Oregon's largest city, you'll drive up the Columbia Gorge, stopping at incomparably beautiful waterfalls along the scenic highway. Later, you'll cross the Bridge of the Gods and drive up the Lewis and Clark Trail to an improbable art museum in a French-style château in the middle of nowhere. Spend the night on the side of Mount Hood.

DAY 14 Today's long drive takes you through a part of the state so sparsely inhabited that the entire population could gather in a high school gymnasium. Along the route are two former boomtowns whose combined populations are now fewer than a hundred people.

Explore the colorful desert of John Day Fossil Beds and view the remains of prehistoric beasts. In the afternoon, drive to Bend.

DAY 15 Spend the morning exploring Lava Lands, a cluster of national forest scenic areas. Drive to the top of a lava cone, see a lava cave, and wander through a lava cast forest. In the afternoon, drive the scenic Cascade Lakes Highway to reach Crater Lake, site of the biggest bang in Oregon's volcanic history and now the deepest lake in the United States.

DAY 16 Devote the daytime to exploring Crater Lake National Park. This evening, watch Shakespeare under the stars at an authentic re-creation of an Elizabethan theater.

DAY 17 As you travel from the mountains to the seashore, stop to visit a vast marble cavern and the northernmost of the California redwood groves.

DAY 18 Today's drive takes you up the southern half of the Oregon coast, where the Pacific Ocean laps broad sandy beaches, crashes upon rocky headlands, and creates giant sand dunes. Other highlights include formal gardens and a wildlife refuge.

DAY 19 Continuing along the northern part of the Oregon coast, you'll discover tide pools, lighthouses, and sea lions. Evening will find you at the mouth of the Columbia River.

DAY 20 Today's drive starts with a nightmarish trip through the heartland of the nation's timber industry but ends sublimely at Olympic National Park's Hoh Rain Forest, one of the world's few temperate zone jungles.

DAY 21 Travel to the extreme northwest corner of the United States to see a unique Indian museum that houses recently discovered artifacts from the dim past of the Northwest coast's native people. Spend another night in Olympic National Park at Lake Crescent.

DAY 22 On the final day of your northwestern adventure, drive high into the Olympic Mountains to hike in the alpine meadows of Hurricane Ridge. Tonight will find you back in Seattle.

DAY 1

SEATTLE

This tour of the Pacific Northwest starts in Seattle, the region's largest city. Travelers who plan to join the itinerary from points farther south, in Oregon or California, skip forward to Day 18 and return to this page when you reach Seattle.

Whether your passion is sightseeing, shopping, urban hiking, or mingling with the natives, downtown Seattle offers plenty to keep you busy for a full day and evening. Start, as the city itself did, at the waterfront and Pioneer Square. Wander through the International District and back to the modern downtown area, where major department stores are dwarfed by bank skyscrapers. From the center of downtown, the monorail to Seattle Center will whisk you back to the future in just 90 seconds.

Suggested Schedule

10:00 a.m.	Begin all-day downtown tour.
10:30 a.m.	Seattle Aquarium.
11:30 a.m.	Pike Place Market and lunch.
12:30 p.m.	Pioneer Square.
1:00 p.m.	Underground Tour.
2:30 p.m.	International District.
3:30 p.m.	Downtown, monorail to Seattle Center.
4:00 p.m.	Seattle Center.
Evening	Whoop it up in downtown Seattle.

Arriving in Seattle

If you're arriving in Seattle by air, SeaTac Airport is 19 miles south of downtown. You can get from the airport to downtown by city bus. If you have more luggage than you can conveniently carry on the bus, rent a car at the airport: an extra day's car rental won't cost much more than taking a taxi downtown. Simply follow the signs to Interstate 5 and drive north to downtown Seattle. If your plans call for renting an RV for this 22-day tour, avoid traffic aggravation and parking problems by waiting until

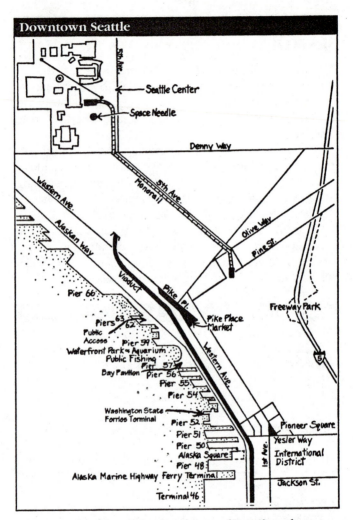

Downtown Seattle

you're ready to leave the Seattle area (Day 3) to do so, and rent a car for these first few days instead. Seattle has hardly any camping facilities.

If you're arriving in Seattle in an RV, you could camp out of town and visit the city as a day trip. Avoid downtown traffic by exiting I-5 at the Seattle Center and riding the monorail downtown. (Even for RV travelers, though, it's more convenient to spend at least the first night in a downtown hotel.)

If you're arriving by Amtrak, the King Street Train Station is at the south end of downtown Seattle, between the International District and Pioneer Square, next to the Kingdome. From here, it's easiest to take a taxi to nearby accommodations and then arrange a car rental for tomorrow.

Seattle

Today's explorations will quickly convince you that Seattle is not your average American big city. Its unique features grew out of a brief, boisterous history. The city got its start in 1852, under the name of Duwamps. In its first decades, most people underestimated this little backwater community and expected Port Townsend, to the north on the far side of Puget Sound, to become the region's major port city. Transcontinental rail service changed that, though, and Seattle's population leaped from 3,500 in 1880 to 45,000 in 1890. In 1896, Seattle's port became the first U.S. shipping link with Japan, and two years later it also became the main departure terminal for the Klondike gold rush to Alaska. By 1910, the city had grown to nearly a quarter of a million, half of its present population.

Within the past few years, Seattle has become known as one of the most desirable American cities in which to live. Californians and others are moving here in droves, and two satellite cities—Bellevue and Everett—rank among the ten fastest growing cities in the nation. Today, the aerospace industry overshadows shipping in Seattle's economy. Besides Boeing (greater Seattle's largest employer), a host of smaller high-tech companies are headquartered here, and inventiveness is viewed as an important aspect of the city's heritage. Color TV was invented here.

Seattle's greatest claim to fame is rain. Many Seattlites take perverse pride in the allegedly lousy weather. A popular T-shirt slogan commemorates the "Seattle Rain Festival—January 1 to December 31." Don't tell anybody, but Seattle's weather is actually quite mild. The annual rainfall, 32 inches, is the same as that of Chicago or Atlanta. Temperatures rarely drop below freezing in the winter or reach 80 degrees in the summer. In July, the sun shines almost every day. It's true that spring, fall, and winter weather tends to be gray and drizzly, but don't cancel a minute of your sightseeing plans just because the sky looks dismal first thing in the morning. It commonly clears up after lunch. Seattlites play golf in the rain, go tent camping, hiking, and fishing in the rain, and drive their sports cars in the rain—convertible top down. Try it (it's only water).

Sightseeing Highlights
▲▲▲**Seattle Waterfront**—It's easy to find the waterfront, downhill from downtown. The Alaska Way Trolley can take you up or down the waterfront for 85 cents ($1.10 during rush hour). Buy a trolley token from the vending machine inside the kiosk at any stop; there are also $1 and $5 change machines.

The points of interest along the waterfront are between Pier 70 (a large old warehouse housing arts and crafts and import shops as well as several small restaurants) on the north and Pier 48 (the Alaska Ferry dock) on the south. Pier 69 is the terminal for Victoria Clippers, high-speed luxury catamarans that carry passengers to Victoria and Vancouver, British Columbia. The Edgewater Inn (see Lodging), with its marvelous mural of orca whales on the north wall, is on Pier 67. Walk south past working ship piers to Pier 59, where the Seattle Aquarium and Omnidome are located. Across the street, the Pike Place Hillclimb takes you up to Pike Place Market.

Pier 57, the next one to the south, is the city's Waterfront Park and public fishing pier.

Pier 56 is the dock for Harbor Tours. The one-hour tours leave at 11:00 a.m. and 12:15, 1:30, 2:45, 4:00, and 5:15 p.m. June through September. In May and October they leave at 12:15, 1:30, 2:45, and 4:00 p.m., and in April they operate Friday through Sunday only. Fares are $11.55 for adults, $5.30 for ages 5 to 12. For more information, call 623-1445.

Pier 54 is the home of two venerable Seattle landmarks. Ivar's Acre of Clams was the clam shack that launched the career of the city's most famous restaurateur, the late Ivar

Haglund. Try the steamed clams or clam nectar and watch the seagulls that flock here in profusion. The birds will cajole you to buy more clams and feed them. (Clever, Ivar.) Ivar's Acre of Clams and adjoining Oyster Bar have long, long lines at lunch hour. Pier 54 is also the new location of Ye Olde Curiosity Shop. A trading post since the Klondike gold rush, the shop has accumulated so many oddities—Indian and Eskimo art and artifacts, Alaskan furs, exotic seashells, South American shrunken heads, and a mummy from the Gila Desert, to mention just a few—that today it's as much a private museum as a curio shop.

Pier 53 is where the harbor's two large fireboats park. On summer Saturdays and Sundays, the fireboats pull out into the bay and spray great arcs of water into the air. Why? So you can photograph them, of course! Next door, on Pier 52, is the Washington State Ferries Terminal. Stop in and pick up the current *Sailing Schedules* and *Fares and Tolls*, two tiny brochures that will provide information that will be helpful later in this itinerary. If you can't wait to cruise Puget Sound, hop on one of the frequent ferries to Bremerton, a 2-hour round-trip for only $3.30 per walk-on passenger. Ferries also go to Winslow on Bainbridge Island for the same price.

Pier 48 is the Alaska Ferry dock. The boat leaves on Fridays for the three-day cruise up the Inland Passage to Skagway. Near the terminal is Alaska Square Park, with a Tlingit Indian totem pole from Haines, Alaska.

▲▲**Seattle Aquarium**—Here you'll find a fine collection of sea creatures, both beautiful and bizarre, including African lungfish, Mexican blind cave fish, electric catfish, a colorful coral reef exhibit complete with sharks, and a "touch tank" where you can fondle sea snails, starfish, and crabs. An aviary houses shorebirds and fish of the Puget Sound area in beach, salt marsh, and rocky shore habitats. Tanks with sea otters and fur seals permit viewing from both above and below the water. Schools of fingerling coho salmon are released from the aquarium into Puget Sound each spring. The small fish imprint on the aquarium's fish ladder and later, as adults, return from the

ocean to spawn, making this the only aquarium anywhere
with a direct, living link to the ocean. The Seattle Aquarium is open daily from 10:00 a.m. to 8:00 p.m. in the
summer, until 6:00 p.m. the rest of the year. Admission is
$6.50 for adults, $4 for ages 6 to 18, $1.50 for ages 3 to 5.
The adjoining Omnidome ($5.95 adults, $4.95 teens 13-18,
$3.95 children 6-12) shows three alternating movies, inclu-
ding one that depicts the eruption of Mount St. Helens, on
a wraparound screen. Upstairs, the Museum of Sea and
Ships also charges a separate admission. Both the Omnidome and the ship museum keep the same hours as the
aquarium.

▲▲▲**Pike Place Market**—Up the Pike Place Hillclimb
stairway, across the street and under the viaduct from the
aquarium, Pike Place started as a farmers' market in 1907.
During the market's revival in the early 1970s, arts and
crafts people started showing their wares side by side with
the vegetable vendors. Today, these artisans complain that
they are being displaced by more commercial retailers and
rising rents, but many continue to survive and prosper.
Pike Place, which has grown beyond its huge three-level
building into Post Alley across the street, is firmly estab-
lished as one of the most fascinating public markets in
any U.S. city. Browse among the stalls selling fresh
seafood (whole salmon and crabs, baby lobsters, fresh
octopus, razor clam meat, and live geoduck—pronounced
"gooey duck"—clams), fresh produce ranging from shii-
take mushrooms to giant artichokes, gourmet food products, and a plethora of gift items, such as figurines hand-
sculpted from Mount St. Helens volcanic ash, Guatemalan
weavings, collectible comic books, watercolor paintings
"made fresh daily," foreign language magazines and news-
papers, and "designer fish" T-shirts. If you've got the urge
to shop 'til you drop, this is the place to do it.

▲▲▲**Pioneer Square**—Once Seattle's "skid row" (in fact,
the term "skid row" derives from the old Skid Road here,
now Yesler Way, where Seattle timber baron Henry Yesler
slid logs through the mud down to his waterfront lumber
mill in the 1880s), the Pioneer Square district underwent
historic preservation and then gentrification to become

today's downtown historic district, brimming with restaurants, theaters, night spots, and art galleries. The original multiethnic waterfront wino population hangs in there despite the invasion of young urban professionals, making Pioneer Square a people-watcher's paradise.

The *sine qua non* of Pioneer Square sightseeing is the Underground Tour that starts at Doc Maynard's in the Pioneer Building on First Avenue facing Pioneer Place Park. When downtown Seattle (today's Pioneer Square district) was devastated by fire in 1899, the ruins were landfilled and the city was rebuilt one story above the former, chronically muddy streets. In the 1960s, while lobbying for historic district status for the area, Pioneer Square Committee Chairman Bill Speidel revealed the existence of what he called "The Forgotten City Which Lies Beneath Seattle's Modern Streets." Seattlites were electrified by this archaeological discovery in their own basement. The chamber of commerce persuaded Speidel to guide tours into the underground on "Know Your Seattle Day" in May 1965, and 500 people took the tour in six hours. Since then, Speidel's tours have become a Seattle institution, acclaimed as the ultimate urban guided tour. Enthusiastic young guides carry on the Speidel tradition: it's not the old brick walls so much as the stories behind them that make this tour outstanding. Eighty- to ninety-minute tours are conducted daily at 11:00 a.m., 2:00 p.m., and 4:00 p.m., as well as 1:00 p.m. on Saturdays and Sundays, and 5:00 p.m. Saturdays only, for $5.50 per adult, $4 for students ages 13 to 17, $4.50 for seniors over age 59, $2.25 for children ages 6 to 12. Reservations are recommended. Call 682-1511 or 682-4646.

Another part of the underground, where you can poke around for free, has been renovated as shops in the Grand Central Arcade, entered through an inconspicuous street-level gate on First Street between Main and Washington. Other Pioneer Square sightseeing highlights include the free Klondike Gold Rush National Historical Park—Seattle Unit at 117 South Main Street, a small museum run by the National Park Service, with exhibits and movies on Seattle's role as the gateway to the Alaskan gold rush of

1898. At Second Avenue and Yesler Way, on the northeast corner of the Pioneer Square district, the Smith Tower was the tallest building in the world outside New York City when it was built in 1914. Today, from its observation deck ($2 for adults, $1 for children under 12), you can look up at the modern downtown skyscrapers, some twice as tall, that dwarf it.

A walking tour of other Pioneer Square historic buildings is published in the free, bimonthly *Pioneer Square Gazette,* available in many shops and restaurants.

▲**International District**—East of the Pioneer Square district, past the Kingdome and King Street Amtrak Station, is Seattle's Asian ethnic neighborhood, where Chinese, Korean, Japanese, Vietnamese, Polynesian, and Filipino influences mingle. On King Street, don't miss Uwajimaya, the largest Japanese supermarket in the United States, where you can shop for bean cakes, sweet Japanese pumpkin, enoki mushrooms, seasoned squid, strange-looking flat fish called *mana katsuo,* yam paste, fried tangle, 80-pound bags of rice, and other items (many of them pink) so cryptically labeled you can make a game out of guessing what they are. Uwajimaya also has an Asian delicatessen and gift items, including an outstanding selection of Oriental cookbooks, cookware, and tea sets, as well as go boards and other Japanese games. Up the hill at 414 Eighth South near the corner of Jackson is the Wing Luke Asian Museum, named after the Chinese city councilman who died in a 1965 plane crash in the Cascades. This outstanding Oriental culture museum features special exhibits from Korea, China, and other Asian Pacific nations, as well as permanent displays ranging from firecrackers to medicinal herbs. Hours are Tuesday through Friday 11:00 a.m. to 4:30 p.m., Saturday and Sunday 12:00 noon to 4:00 p.m. Admission is $2.50 for adults, $1.50 for teens ages 13 to 18, and 75 cents for children. Free on Thursdays.

▲▲**Seattle Art Museum**—This new downtown landmark, located at 100 University Street between 1st and 2nd avenues within easy walking distance of Pike Place Market, contains outstanding collections of Asian, African, Northwest Coast Native American, and contemporary art. The museum is open Tuesday through Saturday from

10:00 a.m. to 5:00 p.m. (Thursdays until 9:00 p.m.), Sunday from 12:00 noon to 5:00 p.m., closed Monday. Admission is $6 for adults, $4 for seniors and students with ID, children under 13 free. Free admission for all on the first Tuesday of each month.

▲**Downtown Seattle**—Seattle's major multistory department stores—Nordstrom, Frederick & Nelson, and the Bon Marché—are all within a block of the downtown monorail station at Fifth and Pine. From there, if you stroll three blocks south on the Fifth Avenue pedestrian mall and a block east on Spring Street to Sixth Avenue, you'll come to Freeway Park, the unique 5.4-acre city park on the concrete roof covering Interstate 5, with gardens, lawns, fountains, waterfalls, and plenty of picnicking downtowners.

▲▲**Ride the Monorail**—Seattle's monorail, constructed as part of the 1962 World's Fair, runs between Seattle Center and downtown every 10 minutes from 10:00 a.m. to 9:00 p.m. (Friday and Saturday until midnight). The fare is 75 cents, and the trip takes just 2 minutes. If you feel like you've done a lot of walking on today's downtown tour, think of the poor monorail operator: the monorail doesn't turn around as it changes directions; instead, it has a driver's seat at each end, so every few minutes the operator must walk to the other end of the coach. In the course of a workday he walks farther than the entire length of the monorail track.

The downtown monorail station is in the upper level of the transit station on Pine Street between 3rd and 4th streets. Below ground level, a 1.3-mile transit tunnel takes Metro buses from other parts of the city to the Pine Street station in the center of downtown. The buses are specially designed to convert from gas to electric power as they enter the underground transit tunnel.

▲▲**Seattle Center**—The site of the 1962 World's Fair has become Seattle's combination town square, playground, and cultural center. Here you'll find the city's most famous landmark, the Space Needle, right next to a roller coaster, a laser light show, an opera house, and a collection of international fast-food places.

The elevator ride to the observation deck atop the 605-

foot Space Needle runs daily from 9:00 a.m. to midnight,
Saturday night until 1:00 a.m., and costs $6 for adults, $5
for seniors, and $4 for children ages 5 to 12.

The Center House, another World's Fair holdover, has
18 fast-food restaurants where you can select anything
from Mongolian steak or Vietnamese *banh bao* to Belgian
waffles, espresso, barbecued ribs, or even Seattle-style
steamed clams. Service is so quick, it puts national chain
fast-food places to shame, and complete meals cost $4 to
$5. The large pavilion in the Center House hosts all kinds
of events. One is a long-standing community tradition:
free international folk-dancing lessons (participate or just
watch) every Thursday at 6:30 p.m. There is a children's
museum downstairs.

The Pacific Science Center, an outstanding teaching
museum for children (of all ages!), has hands-on computer
exhibits, full-size replicas of spacecraft and a space station, and a reconstructed Salish Indian longhouse called
Sea Monster House. An adjoining 8,000-square-foot projec-
tion dome offers astronomy presentations and (for a separate admission) 45-minute laser light shows. Exhibit halls
are open Monday through Friday 10:00 a.m. to 5:00 p.m.,
Saturday and Sunday 10:00 a.m. to 6:00 p.m. Admission is
$6.50 for adults, $5.50 for children ages 6 to 13, and $4.50
for children ages 2 to 5. Senior citizens are admitted free
on Wednesdays.

Fun Forest amusement park rides, including a compact
but thrilling Wild Mouse roller coaster, bumper cars, and
a Ferris wheel, operate June through August daily from
noon to midnight, and April, May, and September on
Friday 7:00 p.m. to midnight, Saturday and Sunday noon
to midnight.

Also at the Seattle Center are the Seattle Children's
Museum, open Tuesday through Sunday, admission $3.50;
the Opera House (call 447-4711 for current opera information, 443-4747 for symphony information); the Children's
Theatre (call 441-1767 for current information); the Coliseum,
where most Seattle rock concerts are held; and the floodlit,
electronically controlled International Fountain.

Lodging

Camping in Seattle is virtually impossible. While RV travelers could camp outside the city (for example, at Dash Point State Park, 5700 Dash Point Road in Federal Way midway between Seattle and Tacoma, or even at Mount Rainier—see Day 11), taking a hotel room in downtown Seattle and parking your motor home until you're ready to leave town means more sightseeing time and fewer traffic hassles.

The best base for exploring downtown Seattle is the **Edgewater Inn** on the waterfront at Pier 67. The location is perfect, within easy walking distance of all downtown sightseeing highlights. Rates range from $109 to $195. Completely transformed in 1989, the Edgewater now bills itself as a "mountain lodge" on the edge of Puget Sound. Fishing from the windows is no longer allowed. For reservations, call (206) 728-7000.

Another great downtown location is the **Inn at the Market**, a French country-style inn at 86 Pine Street, adjacent to Pike Place Market. Rates range from $110 to $175 a night. For reservations, call (206) 443-3600.

If money is no object, Seattle's most elegant small hotel is the **Alexis** at 1007 First Avenue. Once a garage, the 1901 building that houses the Alexis is listed on the National Register of Historic Places. Rates start at about $180. Executive suites, many with fireplaces, rent for $350 a night. Call (206) 624-4844.

At the opposite end of the accommodations spectrum is the **Seattle International Hostel** at 84 Union, (206) 622-5443, with 125 $12 beds (bring your own linen or pay extra) in 22 dormitory rooms. AYH or IYHF membership is required and can be purchased upon arrival at the hostel. Desk registration hours are 7:00 to 9:30 a.m. and 5:00 to 10:30 p.m.; the hostel is closed from 10:00 a.m. to 5:00 p.m., and curfew is at midnight. The hostel is at the entrance to Post Alley, near Pike Place Market and within easy walking distance of Pioneer Square and the International District. It's newly opened, relatively undiscovered, and usually not crowded, though that may change. Advance reservations may be made no less than three

weeks ahead by mailing a deposit of 50 percent of the
charge for your entire stay. Other low-budget downtown
accommodations, in the $25 range for private rooms, are
the **YMCA**, 909 Fourth Avenue, men and women over 18
only, (206) 382-5000, and the **YWCA**, 1118 Fifth Avenue,
women only, (206) 461-4888.

For midrange ($70 to $90) motel accommodations,
try the **Travelodge by the Space Needle** at 200 Sixth
Avenue North, just a short monorail trip from downtown.
For reservations, call (206) 441-7878.

Food

My top dining recommendation in Seattle, not in the
downtown area but worth the drive, is **Ivar's Indian
Salmon House** at 401 NE Northlake Way (on the northeast shore of Lake Union under the freeway bridge, south
of the University of Washington campus), 632-0767. The
specialty is salmon barbecued over alder wood in full
view of the clientele. The interior decor replicates a
Kwakiutl Indian longhouse, log canoes hang from the ceiling, and Indian wood carvings, ranging from museum-
quality artifacts to contemporary Native American art, are
everywhere. There is also a fine collection of turn-of-the-
century photographs of the Coast Salish people, the
whale-hunting Makah of Neah Bay, and the handsome,
nomadic Yakima people. Notice the photograph of Indian
canoes on the Seattle waterfront in 1890. Many of the
photographs are by the late Edward Curtis, North
America's premier photographer of nineteenth-century
Indian life. Ivar's Indian Salmon House was designated as
a historic landmark just one year after it was built. Wait
for a window table and watch the boat traffic on Lake
Union while you eat. The restaurant is open nightly
until 10:00 p.m., Friday and Saturday until 11:00 p.m.
Reservations are not accepted.

The Seattle Center offers two completely different dining
experiences. At the international fast-food restaurants in
the **Center House** (see Sightseeing Highlights, above)
you can feed a family of five for $20. Considerably higher
in both price and elevation is the **Space Needle**

Restaurant, open for breakfast (mid-June through Labor
Day only) 7:30 to 10:00 a.m., lunch 11:00 a.m. to 3:00
p.m., and dinner 5:00 p.m. to 11:00 p.m. (Friday and
Saturday until midnight during the summer). The restaurant revolves once every hour, giving you a 360-degree
panorama of Seattle and Puget Sound while you eat.
Reservations are essential: call 443-2100. Coats and ties are
required for men. A more casual and moderately priced
restaurant is the **Emerald Suite**, midway up the Space
Needle, open the same hours as the Space Needle
Restaurant. Reservations are recommended: call 443-2150.
The elevator ride and observation deck passes are compli-
mentary with a meal at either restaurant.

Your only problem in finding food around Pike Place
Market will be choosing among the overwhelming assortment of international restaurants in all price ranges. A
few, to give you an idea of the range of options, are **Mr.
D's Greek Delicacies**, the **Copacabana Colombian
Restaurant**, **Mee Sum Pastries**, and the market's **Scandinavian Delicatessen**. Or buy fresh fruits, smoked
salmon, steamed clams, and fresh baked goods from the
Pike Place Market food vendors and enjoy a picnic lunch
at Waterfront Park on Pier 57 behind the market.

Perennial restaurant favorites on the Seattle waterfront
include **Ivar's Acre of Clams** and adjoining **Oyster Bar**,
inexpensive and unusual for lunch but very crowded during the noon hour. If liquid refreshment (nonalcoholic) is
what you're after, but Ivar's clam nectar isn't exactly your
cup of tea, head up Broadway from Pike Place Market to
the popular **Gravity Bar**, where you can choose from a
selection of wheatgrass cocktails. Though the taste takes
some getting used to, it's supposed to be outrageously
healthy stuff, sure to leave you bursting with energy for
sightseeing.

The moderately priced **Old Spaghetti Factory** at Elliot
and Broad Street across from Pier 70 is open for dinner
until 9:30 p.m. weeknights, 10:00 p.m. Friday and Saturday, closed Sunday. Reservations are recommended: call
441-7724.

Among the many Asian restaurants in the International District, try the **Nikko Restaurant** (sushi and Japanese-style seafood), 1306 South King Street, dinner only, Monday through Saturday until 10:00 p.m., moderate to expensive, reservations recommended, 322-4641; **Ocean City Restaurant** (dim sum and Peking duck), 609 South Weller, daily 9:00 a.m. to 1:00 a.m., moderate, 623-2333; or **Tai Tung Restaurant** (Chinese), 659 South King Street, daily 10:00 a.m. to 3:00 a.m., inexpensive, reservations recommended, 622-7372.

The most popular after-theater snack spot in town is **Trattoria Mitchelli**, 84 Yesler Way, 623-3883, half a block from Pioneer Square on Yesler. For late-night munchies in a unique ambience, check out **Bob Murray's Dog House**, 2230 Seventh, 624-2741, a cheap and very weird 24-hour cafe right out of 1961, where the clientele includes a strange mix of crusty old seamen and punkers with Day-Glo mohawks.

Nightlife

Seattle's nightclub scene keeps getting better and better. Choices range from jazz at **Dimitriou's Jazz Alley** (2033 Sixth Ave., 441-9729) to ballroom dancing at the **Washington Dance Club** (1017 Stewart St., 628-8939). The city is best known, however, for its alternative rock music venues, where performers from golden oldies such as Paul Revere and the Raiders and the late Jimi Hendrix, to Heart, Nirvana, Soundgarden, Pearl Jam, and rapper Sir Mix-A-Lot all got their starts. Top rock clubs today include the **Fenix Café** (111 Yesler Way, 447-1514), the **Swan Café and Nightclub** (608 First Ave., 343-5288), **Doc Maynard's** (610 First Ave., 682-4649), and the **Central Café** (207 First Ave. S., 622-0209), all at Pioneer Square. Other legendary rock clubs include **The Vogue** (2018 First Ave., 443-0673), **The Off Ramp** (109 Eastlake Ave. E., 628-0232), and **Rockcandy** (1812 Yale Ave., 623-0470).

Seattle is also full of great stand-up comedy clubs. In the Pike Place Market and Pioneer Square area, top venues include the **Comedy Underground** (222 S. Main St., 628-0303), **The Last Laugh Comedy Club** (75 Marion

St., 622-JOKE), and the **Seattle Improv** (1426 First Ave., 628-5000). Unexpected Productions stages competitive improv on Friday and Saturday nights at the **Market Theater** (1428 Post Alley, 781-9273).

While municipal performing arts groups—the ballet, the opera, the repertory theater—appear at venues in Seattle Center, most of Seattle's live theater scene centers around Pioneer Square, which is also the city's main art gallery area. Wine-and-cheese opening receptions are held at most galleries in the district on the first Thursday evening of each month. For complete current events listings, consult the *Tempo* insert to the Friday *Seattle Times*. Concert hot-line information is available from radio stations KEZX (folk and new music, 547-9890) and KISW (rock, 421-5479). Many concerts and events are also posted on the giant bulletin board in Pike Place Market.

AROUND SEATTLE

Seattle also offers a lot to see and do away from the downtown area. Whether to go to the beach, take a woodland hike, or visit museums depends on the weather. Here are my top ten suburban Seattle sightseeing highlights.

Suggested Schedule

Take your pick from the sightseeing highlights listed below.
Explore Seattle until you find it.

Finding Your Way Around Seattle

All of these places can be reached by public bus as well as by car, but driving around Seattle is a memorable experience in itself.

Suburban streets and avenues are numbered. Streets run east-west, while avenues run north-south. The prefix tells you your direction from downtown, and the street number tells you how many blocks. For example, NE 45th Street, which runs past the University of Washington, is east and 45 blocks north of downtown. Avenues in the same area are also designated "NE," so it's up to you to remember that they're the north-south streets. The system sounds easy enough—and it is, as long as you don't drive far enough to cross a county line (at Edmonds or Lynnwood to the north, Tacoma or Puyallup to the south). Then the frame of reference changes, and ascending "N" numbers become descending "S" numbers. Confusing? You bet. The shoreline and distant mountains aren't much help, either, because to the untrained eye, Lake Washington and the Cascade Mountains to the east can look much the same as Puget Sound and the Olympic Mountains to the west, making it easy to convince yourself that you're going in the opposite direction. Don't panic—you're probably not.

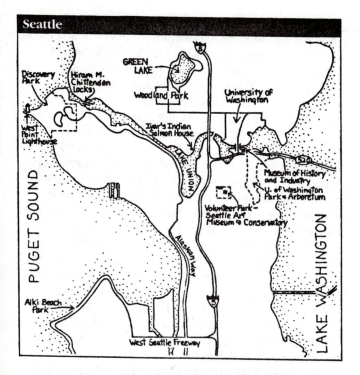

Seattle

While it's easy to get disoriented in the outskirts of Seattle, it's hard to stay lost for very long. Seattle is a long, narrow city, and if you go east or west (taking a street, not an avenue), you're bound to run into a freeway or a shoreline.

Interstate 5, the main north-south freeway, runs right past downtown. Highway 99, a commercial strip and main thoroughfare from the time before freeways were invented, parallels I-5 on the west and becomes the Alaska Way Viaduct above the waterfront. Interstate 405, also north-south, is on the other side of Lake Washington. Highway 520 links the two interstates via the Evergreen Point Floating Bridge, the world's longest (1½ miles).

The fast lanes marked with diamonds on I-5 are for buses and car pools only. If your vehicle contains at least three people, you qualify.

Outdoor Sightseeing Highlights

▲▲**Washington Park Arboretum**—Miles of hiking trails lace this 200-acre forest oasis in the middle of the city, south of Union Bay and the University of Washington campus. The 5,500 species of trees and shrubs are a visual feast, though traffic noise is constantly present. Open daily from dawn to dusk, the arboretum is free except for the Japanese Garden at the south end, which charges $2 for adults and $1 for youths ages 6 to 18 and seniors 65 and over. Foster Island, on the north end of the arboretum, is a natural wetlands area preserved as a wildlife sanctuary on the shore of Lake Washington, with a soggy nature trail that offers good views of birds and boats. The Foster Island nature trail starts at the lower end of the Museum of History and Industry parking lot and at the other end crosses under the Evergreen Point Floating Bridge freeway to join the main arboretum trails. To get to the arboretum from Interstate 5 (northbound from downtown), take Bellevue-Kirkland exit 168 onto Highway 520, cross Montlake Boulevard to Lake Washington Boulevard E, and follow it into the arboretum. Stop first at the visitors center and buy a trail map (25 cents).

▲▲**Discovery Park and Daybreak Star**—Much quieter hiking trails than those in the arboretum can be found at Discovery Park, which even many Seattlites haven't discovered yet. It doesn't sound promising at first: the park, reclaimed from a former military base, adjoins government housing and a sewage treatment plant. Go there and be surprised by 400 acres of forested ravines and broad meadows set aside for hikers only. This is as close to true wilderness as you'll find within Seattle's city limits. The main 2-mile loop trail takes you along Magnolia Bluffs, high sand cliffs that afford a magnificent view of Puget Sound and the Olympic Mountains on a clear day. Side trails lead down to never-crowded beaches on both sides of the point. Also in the park, the Daybreak Star Indian Cultural Center has gallery exhibitions of contemporary fine arts by area Native Americans, as well as special events that range from crafts demonstrations to salmon feasts. Hours are Wednesday through Saturday from 10:00 a.m. to 5:00 p.m., Sunday 12:00 noon to 5:00 p.m. Call 285-4425 for current events. Both the park and Daybreak Star are free. To get there, take the Seattle Center exit from I-5 and, passing Seattle Center, continue on West Mercer Street, which merges into Elliot Avenue West and turns north to become 15th Avenue West. Just before you reach the Ballard Bridge, turn west on Emerson Place to Gilman Avenue, which becomes Government Way and goes right to the park. Daybreak Star signs will help you find the way.

▲**Alki Beach**—Seattle's downtown beach, reached via the West Seattle Freeway just south of downtown, has an early L.A. beachfront ambience, lively on summer days, plus a view of the Space Needle. Don't even think about swimming: the water of Puget Sound is cold enough to cause hypothermia in 15 minutes. Just bask on the sand or flip a frisbee like everybody else. A popular pastime is to bicycle up and down the beachfront, discovering such minor landmarks as the point where Seattle's first European settlers landed and a six-foot replica of the Statue of Liberty was presented to the city by the Boy Scouts. You can rent bicycles across the street from the beach at Alki Bicycle Company. They also offer guided bicycle tours of Seattle.

▲**Hiram M. Chittenden Locks (aka Ballard Locks)**—
The two locks separate Lake Washington and Lake Union from Puget Sound. The water level of the sound changes with the tide as much as 20 feet daily, while the lake level remains a constant 21 feet above sea level, so the locks are needed to raise and lower boat traffic between the lakes and the sound. A U.S. Army Corps of Engineers visitor center explains how the process works. The locks are a boat watcher's paradise. About 100,000 vessels pass through them each year, from small pleasure craft to tugboats and barges. Spend an hour or two here and see the proof that Seattle has more boats per capita than any other U.S. city—one for every six residents. The locks are open to the public from 7:00 a.m. to 9:00 p.m. daily. The

visitor center is open mid-June to mid-September daily from 11:00 a.m. to 8:00 p.m., the rest of the year Thursday through Monday 11:00 a.m. to 5:00 p.m. Free.

▲**Boating on Lake Union**—You can rent a canoe at the University of Washington Boathouse (on Boat Street, at the west edge of campus on the north shore of Portage Bay—take NE Pacific Street west from Montlake Boulevard and turn left at the Hospital sign; Boat Street continues past the campus hospital to the boathouse) and paddle through the ship canal to Foster Island and beyond. Rental rates start at $8 per hour. For sailboat rentals contact the Center for Wooden Boats at 1010 Valley, 382-2628.

Indoor Sightseeing Highlights

▲▲**Volunteer Park**—Palm trees and cacti in Seattle? You'll find them indoors at the Volunteer Park Conservatory, along with banana trees, giant ferns, and more than 1,500 orchids, in five artificial environments ranging from desert to tropical jungle. The conservatory is open daily from 10:00 a.m. to 7:00 p.m. mid-May through mid-September, and from 10:00 a.m. to 4:00 p.m. the rest of the year. Admission is free.

▲**Museum of History and Industry**—More history than industry (the industry part consists of a vintage Boeing mail plane), MOHAI features changing period costume and decor exhibits, an antique-studded replica of a pioneer-era town's wooden storefronts with photographs recounting Seattle's history, and sailing ship displays. The museum is open daily from 10:00 a.m. to 5:00 p.m. Admission is $3 for adults, and $1.50 for children ages 6 to 12 and seniors over 65. To get there, follow the directions above to the Washington Park Arboretum, but turn north on Montlake Terrace for two blocks. MOHAI is on your right (east) just before you reach the bridge.

▲▲**Museum of Flight**—Housed in Boeing's original manufacturing plant, this museum traces the history of aviation from the thirteenth century into the space age. Exhibits include 30 airplanes, many of them suspended from ceiling girders, including a DC-3, a B-7 Flying Fortress, and a B-47 Stratojet. While the museum understandably emphasizes Boeing's role in realizing mankind's dream of flight, special attention is also given to the little-known contributions of Asian and Pacific Rim nations. Hours are from 10:00 a.m. to 5:00 p.m. daily, until 9:00 p.m. on Thursdays. Admission is $6 for adults, $3 for children ages 6 to 15. To get there, take Interstate 5 exit 158 and go northwest one-half mile to 9404 East Marginal Way South.

▲▲**Maritime Heritage Center**—This complex on the Lake Union shoreline features a restored shipyard and the Center for Wooden Boats (1010 Valley St., 382-2628), where handmade boats from around the world are exhibited. It is open Monday through Saturday from 10:00 a.m. to 5:00 p.m. and Sundays from noon to 5:00 p.m. during the summer months, and 12:00 noon to 5:00 p.m. daily the rest of the year. Admission is free. Adjoining the center for wooden boats, the 165-foot turn-of-the-century sailing schooner *Wawona* is open to the public for tours daily from 10:00 a.m. to 5:00 p.m. at Northwest Seaport (1002 Valley St., 447-9800). Admission is by donation.

▲**Nordic Heritage Museum**—If you're Scandinavian, as many Seattlites are, *ja* this one's for you. Exhibits cover fishing, lumbering, and the history of Scandinavian Americans in the Northwest from the eighteenth century to the present. Located at 3014 NW 67th Street in Ballard, the museum is open Tuesday through Saturday 10:00 a.m. to 4:00 p.m., Sunday 12:00 noon to 4:00 p.m. Admission is $3 for adults, $1 for children ages 6 to 16, and $2 for students and seniors.

EXPLORING PUGET SOUND

Take a ferry to the western shore of Puget Sound for the first in a series of minicruises scheduled over the next few days. While today's total driving distance is less than 70 miles, you'll find enough unusual points of interest on the less-populated side of the sound to keep you occupied until dinner time, such as a Salish Indian museum, a New England-style historic town, and the longest island in the United States.

Suggested Schedule

8:00 a.m.	Breakfast, pack, and prepare for long-distance travel.
10:10 a.m.	Seattle-Winslow Ferry.
10:50 a.m.	Arrive in Winslow. Drive to Suquamish.
12:15 p.m.	Visit Suquamish Museum. Picnic in the park by Chief Sealth's grave.
2:00 p.m.	Drive to Port Gamble.
2:30 p.m.	Stroll historic Port Gamble.
3:30 p.m.	Drive to Port Townsend.
5:00 p.m.	Port Townsend-Keystone Ferry.
5:30 p.m.	Arrive at Keystone, Whidbey Island. Drive to Deception Pass State Park or Anacortes.
6:30 p.m.	Camp at Deception Pass, or check into an Anacortes motel or B&B.

Riding the Washington State Ferries

Washington's ferry network carries 7 million vehicles and 17 million passengers each year. The twenty-two vessels, traveling eight routes, are vital highway links: without them, driving from one shore of 10-mile-wide Puget Sound to the other would take all day. Every vehicle that uses the highways—commuter traffic, bicycles, motor homes, log trucks, state police cruisers—also uses these boats.

The key to riding the ferries is a pair of tiny free brochures, *Sailing Schedules* and *Fares and Tolls*. Pick them up the first chance you get—at Seattle's downtown ferry terminal, at a municipal bus schedule rack, upon request at any ferry toll booth, or aboard the ferries—and keep them handy. They are essential information! Ferries run more frequently at busy times of day and on certain days of the week. Service on some routes continues until midnight or later, while on others the last boat leaves as early as 5:00 p.m. Fares, which are not always the same in one direction as the other, cost about 20 percent more during the summer months. Fares for vehicles over 18 feet long (including trailer length) cost almost twice as much, and over 28 feet, the fares are still higher. Schedules change seasonally, so the information listed in this book should only be used as rough guidelines. The fares I've listed are basic summer rates, followed by the lower off-season cost in parentheses, for vehicles less than 18 feet long.

Riding the ferry is easy. Drive down to the ferry dock, pay at the toll booth, and proceed to whichever traffic lane you're told to use. If you have a motor home, camper, or travel trailer, federal law requires that you shut off your propane tank before boarding the boat, and the toll-taker will give you a bright orange sticker to paste across the shut-off valve. When the boat arrives, follow the car in front of you on board, turn off your engine, get out, and lock your vehicle. Upstairs, you'll find a snack bar, lounge areas, indoor and outdoor observation decks, and rest rooms. Have coffee and doughnuts, stroll the deck, feed the seagulls, pretend you're on a cruise ship. Return to your vehicle when you see everybody else doing so, just before the boat touches the dock. Then drive off the boat and find yourself in a new place.

Travel Route: Seattle to Anacortes (66 miles plus ferry travel)

From Seattle's State Ferry Terminal, Pier 52 on the waterfront, the Winslow ferry departs approximately each hour beginning at 6:20 a.m., $6.65 ($5.55 off-season) per vehicle with driver, plus $3.30 per passenger.

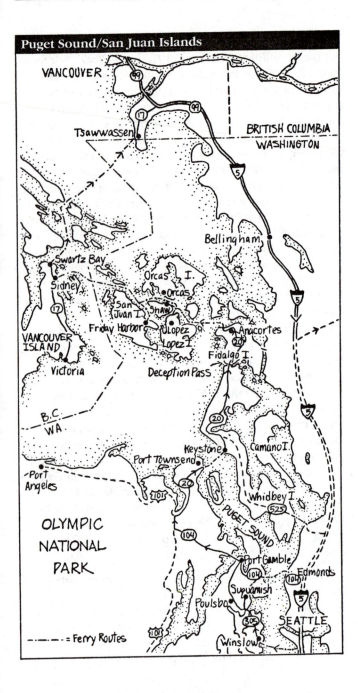

Puget Sound/San Juan Islands

-·-·- = Ferry Routes

Crossing time is 35 minutes. Disembark at Winslow on Bainbridge Island, and drive north on Highway 305 for 6 miles until you reach the Agate Pass Bridge, which links Bainbridge Island with the Kitsap Peninsula. Just over the bridge, turn right and you're in Suquamish.

Alternate route: Most Seattle-area RV rental places are along Highway 99 in the suburb of Lynnwood, 18 miles north of downtown. If you're picking up a vehicle there for your trip, there's no reason to return to downtown Seattle. Instead, take 196th Street westbound for 4 miles to the pleasant little coastal suburb of Edmonds and catch the Kingston ferry, which is the same price as the Winslow ferry and departs more frequently, 30 minutes crossing time. (Following the main itinerary, you'll return via this boat on the evening of Day 22.) Arriving in Kingston, you'll drive 8 miles west to Port Gamble on Highway 104. After seeing the historic town, continue on Highway 104 for another mile and turn south on Highway 3, then east on Highway 305, a total of 13 miles to Suquamish. From there, rejoin the main itinerary route to retrace your tracks.

Everybody: After visiting the Suquamish Museum, go west for 6 miles on Highway 305, then north for 7 miles on Highway 3. When you reach Highway 104, turn right (east) 1 mile to Port Gamble.

Upon leaving Port Gamble, go back 1 mile west on Highway 104 and cross the Hood Canal Bridge (the world's longest floating bridge over tidewater), which takes you to the northeastern corner of the Olympic Peninsula. A road to the right just beyond the bridge follows the shoreline all the way to Port Townsend, rejoining the main route, Highway 20, 5 miles from town.

From Port Townsend, the ferry to Keystone on Whidbey Island departs every hour and a half, but only until 5:00 p.m. Departures are later on Fridays, Saturdays, Sundays, and holidays. The fare is about the same as for the ferry you were on earlier today. The trip lasts 30 minutes.

Whidbey Island is the longest island in the United States (a title it gained in 1985 when the U.S. Supreme Court ruled that Long Island, New York, was actually a peninsula).

It's 55 miles long, with Keystone at the midpoint. When
you get off the boat, you're still on Highway 20—the same
road that took you to Port Townsend. Stay on this highway (it's the only one) north for 30 miles to Deception
Pass and 10 more miles to Anacortes.

Sightseeing Highlights

▲▲**Suquamish Museum**—This museum, operated by
the small neighboring Port Madison Indian Reservation,
exhibits artifacts and photographs of the Puget Sound
Salish people, as well as quotes from tribal elders. The
museum is open daily from 10:00 a.m. to 5:00 p.m. during
the summer months, Wednesday through Sunday 11:00
a.m. to 4:00 p.m. the rest of the year. Admission is $2.50
for adults, $2 for senior citizens, $1 for children ages 2 to
11. Next to the museum is the grave of Chief Sealth, for
whom the city of Seattle was named. Sealth, the leader of
the Duwamish and Suquamish tribes until his death in
1866, was an eloquent orator and spokesman for the
Native Americans of the Northwest. His words upon sign-
ing the Port Elliot Treaty in 1855 seem poignant now:

"When the last Red Man shall have perished, and the
memory of my tribe shall have become a myth among the
White Man, these shores will swarm with the invisible
dead of my tribe, and when your children's children think
themselves alone in the field, the store, the shop, or in the
silence of the pathless woods, they will not be alone. At
night, when the streets of your cities and villages are silent
and you think them deserted, they will throng with the
returning hosts that once filled them and still love this
beautiful land. The White Man will never be alone."

Near Chief Sealth's grave is a city park where once
stood an Indian longhouse, burned by federal agents four
years after Sealth's death to discourage communal living.

▲▲**Port Gamble**—As you stroll through America's oldest
continuously operating lumber company town (founded
in 1853), you may feel as if you've been transported to
nineteenth-century New England. The town's founder,
William Talbot of the Pope and Talbot Lumber Company,

patterned Port Gamble after his hometown, East Machias, Maine. Stately elm trees, brought around Cape Horn as seedlings in the mid-nineteenth century, shade a main street lined with New England-style clapboard homes so perfectly preserved that they look as if they'd been built yesterday. While the town feels like a historical park, most of the houses remain private residences. The general store, stocking items aimed more at the tourist trade than the needs of townsfolk, features a fair selection of gourmet foods and Washington wines. Upstairs you'll find the Sea and Shore Museum, a display of more than 14,000 seashells, which is claimed to be the world's largest collection (open 11:00 a.m. to 4:00 p.m. Tuesday through Sunday from mid-May through mid-September, weekends only the rest of the year; free admission). The lower level of the general store houses the Port Gamble Historic Museum, which recounts the history of the Pope and Talbot Lumber Company (open daily 10:00 a.m. to 4:00 p.m., summer months only; admission is $1 for adults, 50 cents for students and seniors). Even the lumber mill, filling the whole shoreline downhill from the town, has an almost quaint appearance, far different from the heavy-industry ambience of more modern mills you'll see later in this tour.

▲**Port Townsend**—Settled in the 1850s, this town was the largest port on Puget Sound for nearly 40 years. Today, with a population of 6,000, it no longer rivals Seattle as a commercial center, but its historic district features the finest array of Victorian architecture (as well as the most bed and breakfasts per capita) in the state. Panoramic views and beach access can be found at Chetzemolka Park (Jackson Street at Blaine Street) and Fort Worden State Park on the north side of the cape.

▲**Deception Pass State Park**—What deceptively appears from the sea to be one island is actually two (Whidbey and Fidalgo islands), separated by a very narrow strait under towering cliffs. The view westward from the bridge is one of Washington's most familiar seascapes, the subject of countless paintings and photographs. Sunset here is well worth waiting for.

Anacortes—Nationalities can be confusing around this town, which exists primarily as the mainland connection for the San Juans and Canada's Vancouver Island. Anacortes adjoins the largest tulip-growing area outside the Netherlands and has a substantial Dutch population, though which came first—the tulips or the Dutch—is unclear. The town's name—pronounced "Anna-CORT-is"—is a stylized version of "Anna Curtis," the wife of an early real estate promoter who felt that the Fidalgo Island gateway to the San Juan Islands and the Strait of Juan de Fuca ought to have a Spanish-looking name. (Incidentally, the sea captain responsible for the other Spanish names in the area was actually a Greek, Apostolos Valerianos, who adopted the alias "Juan de Fuca" to get a job sailing for the king of Spain.)

Camping
Deception Pass State Park has an attractive forest campground near Cranberry Lake on the north side of the bridge. The last time I camped there, the racket of jet fighters on the approach path to nearby Whidbey Island Naval Air Station was so deafening that I abandoned my campsite in search of an Anacortes motel room. Area residents assured me, though, that the noise problem is not typical and that Deception Pass is the most popular campground around. Check it out for yourself. Campsites cost $8 a night, no hookups.

Lodging
Anacortes has a lot of motels. Reservations are a must during the summer and on weekends. Try the very Dutch **Islands Inn**, 3401 Commercial Avenue, (206) 293-4644, with rooms for $65 to $95. Reservations are essential at charming bed and breakfasts such as the handsome Cape Cod-style **Old Brook Inn**, 530 Old Brook Lane, (206) 293-4768, where doubles rent for $80 a night.

Food
Port Townsend is an excellent place for specialty food shopping. You'll find an impressive selection of regional, international, and gourmet picnic fixin's at **Aldrich's**,

940 Lawrence Street. One of the best bakeries in the Northwest is **Bread and Roses** at 230 Quincy Street. At the **Elevated Ice Cream Company**, 627 Water Street, besides fine quality ice cream you'll find espresso, pastries, handmade chocolates, and other irresistibly fattening goodies.

For dinner in Anacortes, fresh local seafood is the specialty at **Boomer's Landing**, 209 T Avenue next to Wyman's, with a good waterfront view of Guemes Channel. Prices are in the deluxe range. Hours are 11:30 a.m. (noon on Saturday and Sunday) to 10:00 p.m. daily. Reservations are recommended. Call 293-5108. For European (especially Dutch) cuisine, try the moderately priced, outstanding restaurant in the **Islands Motel**. Hours are 5:00 to 10:00 p.m., closed Monday. Reservations are recommended. Call 293-4464.

Important Note on Planning Ferry Travel to the San Juan Islands and Canada

Before you leave Anacortes tomorrow morning, please read all of Days 4, 5, 6, and 7, paying special attention to ferry and lodging information.

This itinerary is designed to help you maximize the experience of ferry cruising through the San Juan Islands and on to the urban corner of British Columbia. Following the plan, you'll set sail for Orcas Island tomorrow morning and spend the day and night there. On Day 5, you'll reboard the ferry and go on to San Juan Island, then get back on the ferry and continue to Victoria, the British Columbia capital, on the island of Vancouver, where you will spend two nights. Finally, you will return to the mainland at the city of Vancouver, British Columbia.

It's a great trip, but a couple of ferry system peculiarities can make it impractical for some travelers. First, the only ferry from Friday Harbor to Victoria leaves in midafternoon. Since camping on San Juan Island is very limited and accommodations can fill up fast, you should avoid stranding yourself on this island overnight unless you have prearranged a place to stay.

Second, when it comes to ferry fares, the trip I outline in the next few days is not the cheapest way to go. The total ferry fares from Anacortes to Victoria with a motor vehicle run just over $40 (about $34 off-season) for car and driver and $7 per additional passenger, and from Victoria to Vancouver, $20.50 for car and driver (more for motor homes) and $4.50 per passenger. The total cost for two people for this four-day ferry cruise is thus about $72. You don't want to take this trip without a vehicle; bicycles (which you can take on the ferry at pedestrian rates) would work fine for sightseeing on Orcas and San Juan islands, but the ferry landings for both Victoria and Vancouver are far outside the cities.

Finally, if you didn't obtain a Canadian insurance coverage card from your agent before you left home (or if the terms of your vehicle rental agreement don't let you take it out of the United States), you should skip Victoria and Vancouver or visit them by public transportation. It's unlikely that anyone will actually check whether your vehicular paperwork is in order, but if it's not and you have an accident, the legal entanglements can be long and expensive.

If you want to travel on the lowest possible budget, or if you haven't arranged lodgings on San Juan Island, consider a different strategy. Take the ferry to Orcas and San Juan islands (total cost about $24 in summer, $20 off-season, and less than $5 per passenger), then return to Anacortes. Eastbound ferry travel from the islands to Anacortes is free. Drive to Vancouver (about 80 miles up Interstate 5, which becomes Highway 99 in Canada).

Later, visit Victoria by the *Victoria Express* passenger ferry from Port Angeles on the Olympic Peninsula (see Day 22). The round-trip cost for foot passengers is $20 per adult and $10 for children under 12. You don't need to take your car, because unlike the San Juan Islands–Victoria ferry, the one from Port Angeles docks right in downtown Victoria.

Still, I think the four-day San Juans–Victoria–Vancouver cruise I describe in Days 4 through 7 is well worth a little extra expense and advance planning. As an international cruise with varied, exotic ports of call, this trip is so satisfying that before you're finished, you'll completely forget you're never more than 150 miles from Seattle.

ORCAS ISLAND

Misty, remote, forested, and wild, the cluster of islands at the northern end of Puget Sound will tug at your imagination as you glide among them on the San Juan ferry, one of America's best cruise bargains.

Suggested Schedule	
7:20 or	
8:50 a.m.	Ferry from Anacortes to Orcas Island.
9:50 a.m.	Arrive at Orcas.
10:00 a.m.	Drive to Moran State Park.
11:00 a.m.	Get a campsite, or drive on to Doe Bay Village Resort. Picnic.
Afternoon	Explore Moran State Park.

The San Juan Islands

Though just about 65 miles straight-line distance from downtown Seattle, the San Juan Islands are a world apart from the freeways, suburbs, and shopping malls of the mainland. The number of islands in the San Juans is variously estimated at anywhere from 172 to over 700, depending on where the line is drawn between an "island" and a "rock." Most of the islands can only be reached by small boat. They include privately owned islands, many with luxurious vacation homes, as well as state parks, federal wildlife refuges, and lighthouse reserves. Annual rainfall in the San Juans is 29 inches, significantly less than in Seattle.

The ferry trip through the San Juans is the most scenic cruise of the Washington State Ferry System. The islands are a popular summer tourist destination, and on weekends and holidays from Memorial Day to Labor Day motorists may wait in line for several hours to board a ferry, then spend the rest of the day searching for a room or campsite. For this reason, I suggest visiting the islands during the middle of the week and leaving Anacortes as early in the morning as possible, breakfasting on the ferry.

During the summer season, it's best to reserve a room in advance if you plan to spend the night on San Juan Island (Day 5): there are very few campsites there.

Ferry Travel from Anacortes to Orcas Island

Note: all San Juan Islands/Sidney, B.C., ferries run Monday through Saturday only. If today, tomorrow, or the next day is a Sunday, you'll have no choice but to adjust your itinerary and stay where you are on that day.

At Anacortes, board the San Juan Islands ferry for Orcas Island. Unless you have lodging reservations on Orcas Island, be at the ferry dock early to make sure you get a space on the next boat—particularly on summer weekends, when it's much busier than any other Washington State ferry ever is, even during rush hours. At those times, a wait of three hours in line is common. Eight ferries go daily to Orcas Island; plan to take an early one—6:35, 7:20, or 8:50 a.m. After the 8:50 a.m. departure, there isn't another ferry to Orcas until 11:15 a.m. The fare is $16.60 ($13.85 off-season) for the car and driver, plus $4.65 per passenger. Crossing time from Anacortes to Orcas is one hour. (Earlier ferries, but not the 8:50, stop at Lopez and Shaw islands, 20 minutes and 10 minutes before arriving on Orcas.)

Lopez Island is mainly an agricultural island, which most tourists bypass. There are two public parks on Lopez—Odlin County Park and Spencer Spit State Park. Both are on the north shore of the island, near the ferry dock, and both have campsites. Persistent rumors, confirmed by occasional newspaper reports of big busts, suggest that Lopez Island is the marijuana-growing capital of Washington. Visitors to the island will find no evidence of this low-key greenhouse farming, but minding one's own business is wise around here.

Shaw Island, the smallest of the four islands you can reach by ferry, has 100 residents, a combined general store and post office, a little red schoolhouse on the National Register of Historic Places, and a small county park on the south shore.

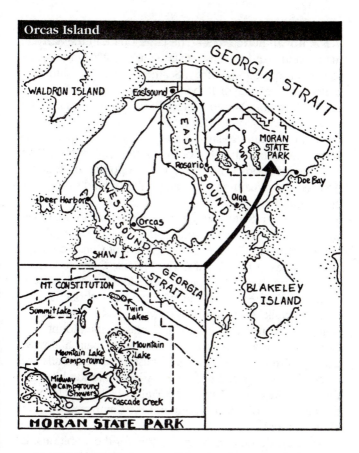

Orcas Island, the largest of the San Juans, is almost two separate islands, linked only by a narrow neck where Eastsound, the largest town, is situated. From the tiny port village of Orcas on the western half of the island, where you get off the ferry, it's an 8½-mile drive to Eastsound on the main road, known as the Horseshoe Highway. Then the road turns back south across the eastern half of the island, 4½ miles more to the entrance of Moran State Park. Following the signs to the park, you can't get lost. Ignoring the signs, you can't get very lost anyway—it's a small island.

Sightseeing Highlights

▲▲▲**Moran State Park**—The largest park in the San Juan Islands, and the largest state park in Washington, was a gift to the public from Seattle industrialist, shipbuilder, and ex-mayor Robert Moran. In 1905, suffering from exhaustion, Moran was told by doctors that he had only six months to live. He retired to Orcas Island to spend his remaining days—and lived there for the next 38 years. Moran bought most of the eastern half of the island, built the luxurious Rosario Resort on a portion of it, and donated the remaining 13 square miles of land to the state of Washington.

While Moran State Park has virtually no coastline, it has two large lakes (Cascade Lake and Mountain Lake), the highest mountain in the San Juans (Mount Constitution), and 26 miles of hiking trails. The 2½-mile Cascade Loop Trail around the far side of Cascade Lake leaves from the roadside at either end of the lake and takes about 1½ hours to walk. A quarter-mile downhill walk, from the pullout on your right about half a mile up the Mount Constitution road from where it leaves the main highway, takes you through lush ancient forest to Cascade Falls and a series of other small waterfalls. A long lakeside hike is the 4-mile Mountain Lake Loop Trail, which starts from the ranger's cabin near Mountain Lake Campground; allow 3 hours.

The ultimate hike in the park, only for the ambitious, is the Twin Lakes Trail, which branches off the Mountain Lake Loop at the north end of the lake, leads 2 miles to a pair of small secluded lakes (passing an abandoned cabin said to have been a hideout for draft dodgers from the Civil War), and then climbs another 4 miles to the 2,160-foot summit of Mount Constitution. Allow all day for this long hike, or 5 to 6 hours one-way if you can arrange to have someone drive to the summit and pick you up there.

The easy way to reach the top of Mount Constitution is to drive up the steep, narrow, paved road. Whether you hike or drive, don't miss the trip to the summit, where you'll find the best possible bird's-eye view of the San

Juan Islands. You can also see the mainland coastline, the Cascade Mountains, Whidbey and Fidalgo islands, Vancouver Island, and, on an exceptionally clear day, Mount Rainier and the Olympic Mountains far to the south. The tower at the summit is a replica of a twelfth-century Eastern European watchtower. It was built in 1935-36 by the Civilian Conservation Corps, using stone that was quarried on another island, brought to Orcas Island by boat, and hauled all the way up the mountain.

While in Moran State Park, watch carefully and constantly for bald eagles. Most Americans never have a chance to see this endangered bird, our nation's symbol, flying free. More likely than not, you will spot one if you look here or on San Juan Island. The San Juan Islands are home to the highest permanent concentration of bald eagles in the world: at least 30 of these magnificent birds are known to live here year-round.

Camping

Moran State Park has a total of 136 campsites (no hookups) in several campgrounds at Cascade Lake and one at Mountain Lake. This is one of the few Washington State Parks camping areas where you can (and should) make reservations if you'll be visiting between May 1 and Labor Day. Reservation applications are available from the Washington State Parks and Recreation Commission, 7150 Clearwater Lane, KY-11, Olympia, WA 98504, (206) 753-2027. Without an application form, you can make a reservation by sending your name, address, and phone number, number of people in your party, arrival date, number of nights you will stay, and the type and size of your camping unit, along with a $4 reservation fee and $8 first night's camping fee, to Moran State Park, Star Route, Box 22, Eastsound, WA 98245-9603. If you are hoping to camp at the park without a reservation during the summer months, call the state parks campground hot line, (800) 562-0990, to check on availability before leaving the mainland. At any time of year, plan to arrive early and locate a campsite first thing upon arrival.

Lodging

Rosario Resort was built by the man who created Moran State Park. Near the park entrance, Rosario has waterfront views, tennis courts, a beach, and a spa, as well as bike and moped rentals. Its villas surround Robert Moran's original 1906 mansion. Rooms range from $63 ($95 on weekends) to $195 single or double. For reservations, call (206) 376-2222.

A different kind of Orcas Island resort is **Doe Bay Village**, on the southeast shore beyond Moran State Park and Olga. Cottages start at $30, and there is also a hostel dormitory ($9.50 for AYH members, $12.50 for non-members) and a campground (sites $8.50 per night). Best of all are the hot mineral baths and steam sauna ($3 for guests, $5 for nonguests). Reservations are essential for both cottages and the hostel. Write Doe Bay Village, Star Route, Box 86, Olga, Orcas Island, WA 98279, or call (206) 376-2291 or 376-4755. Guided kayak trips ($25) to the national wildlife refuge provide a special experience. The 60-acre facility also has a natural foods café and a general store leaning toward health foods.

Near the ferry dock in Orcas is the historic Victorian **Orcas Hotel**. Famed for its fine restaurant, it operates as a bed and breakfast with rooms starting at $69 double. For reservations, write P.O. Box 155, Orcas, WA 98280, or call (206) 376-4300. Among the other Orcas Island B&Bs, I recommend **Turtleback Farm Inn**, an 1890s farmhouse at Route 1, Box 650, Eastsound, WA 98245, (206) 376-4914. Rates range from $70 to $155 a night.

Food

The dining rooms at **Rosario Resort** and the **Orcas Hotel**, both serving moderate to expensive breakfasts, lunches, and dinners daily, are among the island's top restaurants. **Christina's**, on Horseshoe Highway in Eastsound, is the most famous restaurant on the island—open 5:00 to 9:30 p.m. daily, 376-4904. Also in Eastsound: **Bilbo's Festivo** on North Beach Road is said to be one of Washington's best Mexican restaurants, open for dinner only from 5:00 p.m. on, closed Monday, 376-4728; and **La**

Famiglia Ristorante is a popular Italian restaurant, open 11:30 a.m. to 2:30 p.m. and 5:00 to 9:00 p.m., closed Sunday, 376-2335. Both are moderately priced.

The country-style grocery store in Orcas, a block down the hill from the ferry dock ramp, has a good selection of picnic and camping food, from simple staples to gourmet treats. **Westsound Store**, on Crow Valley Road in Westsound, has a great delicatessen.

SAN JUAN ISLAND

When you hop from Orcas to Friday Harbor, you'll quickly discover that while the two largest islands in the San Juans are only a few miles apart, they're as different as can be. Among the experiences today holds in store for you are a visit to a whale museum, a whale-watching picnic lunch, and a stroll on the site of one of the longest—and quietest—"wars" in U.S. history.

Because the only ferry from Friday Harbor to Vancouver Island runs in midafternoon, most visitors will find it more convenient to stop for a few hours on San Juan Island, then continue on to Canada and spend the night in Victoria. This section includes lodging information for those who wish to spend extra time on San Juan Island.

Suggested Schedule

Early!	Return to the Orcas ferry dock and get in line.
7:35 or 8:35 a.m.	Ferry to Friday Harbor, San Juan Island. Breakfast on the ferry.
8:10 or 9:15 a.m.	Arrive at Friday Harbor.
9:30 a.m.	Visit English Camp.
10:30 a.m.	Whale-watch at Lime Kiln State Park.
11:30 a.m.	Visit American Camp.
1:00 p.m.	Return to Friday Harbor. Visit the Whale Museum.
3:30 p.m.	Board the ferry to Sydney on Vancouver Island.
5:00 p.m.	Land at Sydney. Drive south to Victoria.
5:30 p.m.	Check into your Victoria accommodations.
Evening	Dinner and nightlife.

Travel Route: Orcas Island-San Juan Island-Victoria (ferry)

Ferries leave Orcas for Friday Harbor on San Juan Island at 7:35 a.m., 8:35 a.m., 10:20 a.m., and three other times in the afternoon and evening. Take the earliest ferry you can, since camping and other accommodations are a problem on San Juan Island. The interisland fare is $7.75 ($6.50 off-season) per vehicle, no additional charge for passengers. The crossing time is approximately 40 minutes. Toll-taking is a relaxed affair at Orcas; on slow days, instead of paying at the gate, you may have to buy a ferry ticket at the state liquor store, a block down the hill and across the street from the grocery store.

(Evening ferries from Friday Harbor to Anacortes leave at 6:50, 7:55, and 10:00 p.m.)

The only ferry from San Juan Island to Sidney on Vancouver Island leaves Friday Harbor at 3:30 p.m. (Note: Another ferry leaves Anacortes at 8:00 a.m. and Orcas at 9:15 a.m. but bypasses San Juan Island to arrive at Sidney at 11:00 a.m.) The fare is $15.90 ($13.25 off-season) for vehicle and driver, plus $2.25 per passenger. Sailing time from Friday Harbor to Sidney is about 1 hour 25 minutes.

San Juan Island, in the United States, is actually north of the city of Victoria, British Columbia. The ferry, traveling just about due west, lands at the tiny port town of Sidney, about 18 miles north of the city on a peninsula. Follow Highway 17 south, and it will take you directly into downtown Victoria as Blanshard Street. You'll find convenient parking just north of the Empress Hotel.

To visit Victoria's premier sightseeing attraction, Butchart Gardens, on your way into the city (most other sights are located in the downtown area), turn off Highway 17 on either McTavish Road or Mt. Newton Cross Road and drive across the peninsula to Highway 17A (West Saanich Road), which takes you to Benvenuto Road and Butchart Gardens. Upon leaving the gardens, continue south on Highway 17A. It joins Highway 17 a few miles north of downtown.

Sightseeing Highlights
▲▲**Whale Museum**—Whale watching has become big business all along the U.S. coastline in the past few years, proving that helping tourists look at the earth's largest creatures is more lucrative than killing whales ever was.

If the appeal of waiting for hours for the chance to see a cetacean surface and breathe has been lost on you up to now, this casual, almost hippie-ish museum is likely to convert you. It is probably the most comprehensive museum in the world devoted entirely to whales. Exhibits include whale skeletons, whale art, whale migration maps, whale videos, whale voice recordings, and lots more. A reading area contains a collection of articles and books on whales that you could spend the rest of your life perusing. On one wall, a chart traces the genealogy of every pod (family) of orcas (killer whales) that swims in the Strait of Juan de Fuca, with photographs that identify each individual orca by its unique fin markings. The museum, located at 62 First Street a couple of blocks from the ferry dock, is open daily from 10:00 a.m. to 5:00 p.m. Memorial Day weekend through September, 11:00 a.m. to 4:00 p.m. the rest of the year. Admission is $3 for adults, $2.50 for students and seniors, $1.50 for children ages 6 to 11.

If you have extra time, the Whale Museum operates wildlife and whale-watching cruises from May through September on the *Western Prince* tour boat to see harbor seals, bald eagles, and sea birds and search for orcas, minke whales, and porpoises. Four-hour cruises leave at 1:00 p.m. on Saturdays, Sundays, and Mondays and cost $40 per adult, $29 for children ages 12 to 17, and $20 for children age 11 and under. Six-hour extended search cruises leave at 11:00 a.m. on Fridays only, $50 per adult and $30 plus 50 cents per year of age for children under 18, including lunch. All cruises return at 5:00 p.m. and include admission to the Whale Museum. For information and reservations, call (206) 378-5313 or (800) 757-6722.

▲▲**San Juan Island National Historical Park**—Situated midway between the United States and Canada, San Juan Island got its chance to become a historical footnote in 1859, when American farmer Lyman Cutlar shot a British pig from the Hudson's Bay Post that was rooting in his potato patch. It was the first crime ever committed on the island. When British authorities came to bring Cutlar to Victoria and justice, they touched off a twelve-year dispute over whether the San Juans belonged to Canada or the

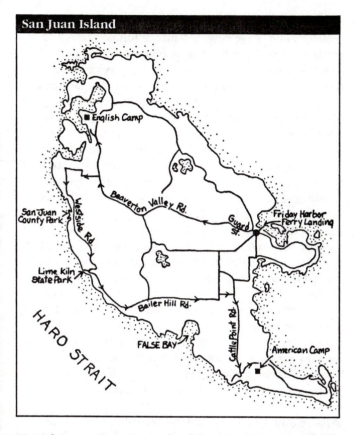

San Juan Island

United States. Opposite ends of the island were occupied by 461 U.S. Marines and more than 2,000 British soldiers. A sign at English Camp says the confrontation "brought England and the United States to the brink of war," though the only shot fired was the one that killed the pig. Acting as mediator, Kaiser Wilhelm I of Germany, Queen Victoria's cousin, proved his impartiality by deciding that the island was U.S. territory—which is why you don't have to exchange currency here. Admission to all park units is free.

English Camp—On lovely Westcott Bay at the west side of the island, reached by following Beaverton Valley Road (the main cross-island road from Friday Harbor), this site has three restored buildings from the British occupation on 530 landscaped acres. One building contains an interpretive center. Park rangers tend the formal English gardens originally cultivated by officers' wives and, on summer weekends, don nineteenth-century uniforms for historical presentations. There are no camping facilities.

American Camp—On Cattle Point at the southeastern tip of the island, this site is twice as large as English Camp. There's little left in the way of historical structures, but along a ¾-mile walking trail you'll find a series of signs recounting the story of the Pig War and get a feel for what U.S. soldiers must have experienced as they defended this lonely little corner of the country—and, in so doing, completely missed the Civil War.

▲**Lime Kiln State Park**—On the west side of the island, midway between English Camp and American Camp, Lime Kiln State Park is reputed to be the best place to watch for orcas. On the average, one sighting is reported each day. The orca's large dorsal fin (up to six feet tall) makes it easier to spot than most other whales, and its loud breathing can be heard for a great distance. Orcas, as well as minke whales, are spotted here throughout the year since they do not migrate, but summer is the peak time to watch for them. Orcas travel in pods, so if you spot one, keep looking and you're likely to glimpse the rest of the family.

▲**False Bay**—Farther down the west shore from Lime Kiln State Park toward American Camp, follow False Bay Road to this shallow, circular bay, which becomes a mud flat at low tide, revealing a weird and wondrous assortment of marine life, including clingfish, bright orange ribbon worms, and purple crabs. The bay is a biological study area owned by the University of Washington, but you're welcome to don galoshes or squishy sneakers and slog around to your heart's content; just don't remove or kill anything living there.

Camping
San Juan Island has just one tiny public campground, 14 units at **San Juan County Park** on the west side of the island at Smallpox Bay (so named because it was the site

of a tragedy that destroyed the island's Indian population when they plunged into the frigid water to cool the small-pox fever—and died of pneumonia instead; nevertheless, the bay is beautiful). To get there, take Beaverton Valley Road across the island from Friday Harbor, turn left on West Side Road, and follow it around several corners to the park. Camping costs $10. The park sometimes closes due to water shortages during the peak of the summer tourist season.

On Vancouver Island, the most convenient public camp-ground, about 18 miles from town but midway between the Sidney and Swartz Bay ferry docks, is **McDonald Provincial Park**, off Highway 17. There are no hookups or showers. Camping costs $8 a night.

Lodging

What San Juan Island lacks in camping facilities is more than compensated for by its fine selection of B&Bs. You need advance reservations at any of them. Friday Harbor B&Bs include the **Tucker House**, $85 and up ($10 less October-May), 260 B Street, and the **San Juan Inn**, about $80 a night, P.O. Box 776. Elsewhere on the island are **Moon & Sixpence**, a Beaverton Valley farmhouse with rates from $80 to $95, 3021 Beaverton Valley Road, Friday Harbor, (206) 378-4138; the **Trumpeter Inn**, $85 to $95, 420 Trumpeter Way, Friday Harbor, (206) 378-3884; and the **Hillside House Bed & Breakfast**, $65 to $145, chil-dren over 10 welcome, no pets, 365 Carter Avenue, Friday Harbor, (206) 378-4730. Friday Harbor also has an AYH youth hostel in the historic **Elite Hotel**, 35 First Street, (206) 378-5555. Dormitory beds cost $7.50 for members, $9 for nonmembers. The old hotel also has a few private rooms at $25.

In Victoria, the **Empress Hotel** (see Day 6 Sightseeing Highlights) offers antique-furnished rooms, some with harbor views, from about $170 to $265 a night mid-April to mid-October, as low as $119 a night off-season, with suites costing as much as $600 a night. For reservations, call (604) 384-8111 or toll-free (800) 828-7447 from the United States, (800) 268-9420 from Canada.

A more affordable historic lodging is the **Dominion Hotel**, at the corner of Yates and Blanshard a couple of blocks west of the Maritime Museum. Dating back to 1876, the Dominion is Victoria's oldest hotel and has an antique-filled lobby and modern guest rooms. Rates are $95 to $115 during the summer months, in the $50 range off-season. Call (604) 384-4136 or toll-free (800) 663-6101.

Victoria has a wealth of English-style bed-and-breakfast inns, many in historic houses. Typical rates are in the $100-a-night range. Try the **Battery Street Guest House**, 670 Battery Street, Victoria, BC V8V 1E5, (604) 385-4632, or the **Captain's Palace Inn**, 309 Belleville Street, Victoria, BC V8V 1X2, (604) 388-9191. For other bed-and-breakfast possibilities, contact the All Season Bed & Breakfast Agency, Box 5511, Station B, Victoria, BC V8R 6S4, (604) 595-2337.

Simple budget accommodations can be found down-town at the **James Bay Inn**, a converted 1907 mansion that was once the home of Victoria's best-known painter, Emily Carr. Rates are $30 to $40 a night with shared bath, about $50 a night with private bath. The inn is at the corner of Government Way and Toronto Street, a few blocks south of Thunderbird Park. Call (604) 384-7151.

The **Victoria Hostel** (IYH), at 516 Yates Street near the waterfront, offers dormitory accommodations at $10 per person including kitchen privileges, a TV room and library, and laundry facilities. Call (604) 385-4511.

Food

Picnicking is your best bet on San Juan Island. English Camp, San Juan County Park, and American Camp are all good picnic spots, but I'd choose Lime Kiln State Park, where you can whale-watch while you eat.

Down Riggers on Front Street, 378-2700, is a good steak and seafood restaurant with a waterfront view, open for lunch and dinner. Or how about pizza at the **Friday Harbor Bistro**? It's in the Elite Hotel, along with the youth hostel, but not cheap. It's open 10:00 a.m. to

9:00 p.m., 378-3076. Other Friday Harbor favorites include the **Café Biset** and the **Springtree**. Both feature fresh local specialties.

Your best bet for a memorable lunch in Victoria is at **Butchart Gardens**, where meals are served in several price ranges: a gourmet dining room, a moderately priced greenhouse restaurant, and in the summer months an outdoor coffee bar.

For elegant (and expensive) dining this evening, you might try the main dining room at the **Empress Hotel.** Call 384-8111 for reservations. The hotel also has a more casual and moderately priced coffee shop. Behind the Empress, in a wing of the Crystal Garden (a tropical rain forest greenhouse complete with monkeys and exotic birds that operates as a commercial tourist attraction), is **Rattenbury's**, a moderately priced steak and seafood restaurant with both indoor and outdoor tables, open daily from 11:30 a.m. to 10:00 p.m., weekends until 11:00 p.m. Call 381-1333 for reservations.

The **James Bay Tearoom**, behind the Parliament buildings at 322 Menzies Street, offers reasonably priced, traditional English fare Monday through Saturday from 7:00 a.m. to 9:00 p.m. and Sunday from 9:00 a.m. to 9:00 p.m. Afternoon tea is served Monday through Saturday from 1:00 to 5:00 p.m., with high tea Sunday from 2:00 to 5:00 p.m. The decor consists of innumerable photos of Great Britain's royal family along with some royal wedding mementos. Call 382-8282 for dinner reservations.

Or dine quite affordably at **Fogg n' Suds**, 711 Broughton Street (about 3 blocks north and 2 blocks east of the Empress), one of a chain of popular pub-style restaurants opening throughout the Greater Vancouver-Victoria area. The "Fogg" part of the name is for Phileas Fogg, hero of Jules Verne's *Around the World in 80 Days*, and reflects the menu choices, each representing a different nationality. The "Suds" part is for beer—your choice of more than 250 different brands. Open daily from 11:00 a.m. until 1:30 a.m., closes at midnight on Sunday.

Entering Canada

The boundary between the United States and Canada is the longest undefended border on earth. Normally, crossing it is easy, especially when entry points are busy, as they are at the Vancouver Island ferry dock and on the interstate highway that links the two largest cities in the Pacific Northwest. Unless you're so suspicious-looking that you are routinely detained for interrogation at airport security checks, you will be waved through after a few quick questions about your citizenship, the purpose of your visit, and whether you are carrying any alcohol, tobacco, fruit, vegetables, or firearms. Vehicle or baggage searches are uncommon, and you probably will not be required to show any documents. Still, it's a good idea to have the legally required paperwork in your possession.

U.S. citizens do not need a passport, visa, or tourist card to enter Canada. Citizens of other nations must have a valid passport unless they are permanent legal residents of the United States, in which case a green card will do. Naturalized U.S. citizens should carry their naturalization certificates, and all U.S. citizens should carry birth certificates or other proof of citizenship. A voter registration card is acceptable. If you are traveling with a dog or cat, you must have a current rabies vaccination certificate (not just the collar tag) for the animal.

Besides your vehicle registration (and, if it is not registered in your name, written permission from the owner to use the vehicle in Canada), you must have a Canadian Non-Resident Inter-Provincial Motor Vehicle Liability Insurance Card. Get one from your insurance agent before leaving home.

While there are very few restrictions on personal effects you can bring into Canada, you are limited to one carton of cigarettes and either 40 ounces of liquor or wine or 24 cans of beer per person. Crossing into Canada with illegal drugs in your possession, including any amount of marijuana, means prison if you're caught. If you smoke cigarettes, it's a good idea to bring a supply along from the United States instead of planning to buy them in Canada, where they cost at least twice as much—often $5 Canadian (US$4.25) a pack.

You can exchange currency at any bank or, for a slightly less favorable rate, at most hotels. A Canadian dollar is worth about 85 U.S. cents; a U.S. dollar is worth about $1.18 Canadian. Practically any business in Victoria or Vancouver will accept U.S. currency, but prices will be the same whether you pay in U.S. or Canadian dollars (you don't get credit for your U.S. dollars being worth more), so you save 15 percent by using Canadian money. Don't exchange more money than you expect to spend. Back on the U.S. side of the border, few businesses will accept Canadian money, and you can only exchange it back at a bank or major airport.

The border check upon reentering the United States from Canada is equally easy. If you have spent at least 48 hours in Canada, you can bring back up to $400 per person worth of goods you bought there without paying import duties. However, if you were in Canada less than 48 hours, you can only bring back $25 worth of purchases per person without being taxed. (Since there is no document to show when you entered Canada, the U.S. officer will take your word for how long you were there.) The kinds of contraband that you cannot legally bring into the United States are numerous and well known: drugs, endangered species products, pornography, subversive publications, switchblade knives, and so on; but such items are generally harder to find in Canada than in the United States anyway. The most common item readily available in Canada that is illegal to bring back is Cuban cigars.

DAY 6

VICTORIA

Today's itinerary offers a chance to explore Victoria, the very British capital of British Columbia. You'll find it unlike any other place on North American shores. Among the pleasures that this stately, dignified frontier city holds in store are visits to Parliament, a Scottish castle, and Canada's most famous formal gardens.

Suggested Schedule

9:00 a.m.	Eat a leisurely breakfast.
10:00 a.m.	Call Butchart Gardens for lunch reservations. Then take a stroll around downtown Victoria. Visit Parliament and the Empress Hotel.
12:00 noon	Drive to Butchart Gardens. Have lunch and stroll through the gardens.
2:30 p.m.	Return downtown to visit the Royal British Columbia Museum and nearby Thunderbird Park.
5:00 p.m.	In favorable weather during the summer months, take a walk to Craigdarroch Castle for an early evening tour.
Evening	Dinner

Orientation

The capital of British Columbia, Victoria (pop. 250,000) got its start in 1843 as the western headquarters of the Hudson's Bay Company, the British fur trading concern that explored and exploited Canada from coast to coast. Originally called Fort Camosun, in 1849 its name was changed to Victoria in honor of the British queen when Vancouver Island became a crown colony. Twenty-two years later, when British Columbia was declared a province of Canada, Victoria—then the largest settlement on the West Coast—was made the provincial capital. Climate was then, as it is now, a Victoria virtue: sheltered by the mountains of the Olympic Peninsula, the city receives only 27 inches of rainfall a year—less than Seattle and less than half as much as Vancouver.

Through the twentieth century, Victoria has existed in the economic shadow of its much larger neighbor, Vancouver, across the Strait of Georgia. In many ways, the island capital seems bound by British colonial tradition and bypassed by time. In fact, many residents proudly claim that Victoria is more British than Great Britain. Victoria capitalizes on its quaintness, and the tourist trade rivals government as a major reason for the continued existence of this city of tea shops and doubledeckers, bagpipers and horse-drawn carriages, formal gardens and stately Tudor mansions. Commercial attractions have sprung up in profusion, among them Undersea Gardens, Sealand of the Pacific, Fable Cottage Estate, the Classic Car Museum, and the Royal London Wax Museum (yes, Chuck and Di are represented there), but whether you choose to patronize these places or ignore them, you won't run out of sights to marvel at in this unique city. It's like prewar London—with totem poles.

Sightseeing Highlights

▲▲▲**Butchart Gardens**—Thanks to the mild climate and bountiful rainfall, the Pacific Northwest boasts more than its share of the finest formal gardens in North America, and no other is as large, elegant, or worldfamous as Butchart Gardens. Strangely, this 50-acre horticultural wonder got its start as an industrial cement quarry. In 1904, when the quarry was abandoned, Jenny Butchart, the owner's wife, decided to start reclaiming the eyesore by hauling in topsoil in a horse-drawn wagon and landscaping it. The original garden is now known as the Sunken Garden. Over the next two decades, Jenny added a Japanese garden, an English rose garden, and an Italian garden, enhancing them with fountains, ponds, and waterfalls and introducing waterfowl and peacocks. As word of her gardens spread, the Butcharts abandoned the cement business and devoted their full efforts to developing the tourist attraction. Today, nearly a century later, the gardens are owned and maintained by the Butcharts'

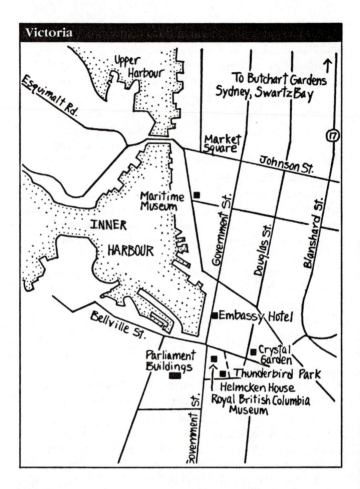

Victoria

Upper Harbour

Esquimalt Rd.

To Butchart Gardens
Sydney, Swartz Bay

⑰

Market Square

Johnson St.

Maritime Museum

INNER

HARBOUR

Government St.

Douglas St.

Blanshard St.

Bellville St.

Embassy Hotel

Crystal Garden

Parliament Buildings

Thunderbird Park
Helmcken House
Royal British Columbia Museum

Government St.

grandson. Butchart Gardens contain over one million plants, including 700 varieties of flowers that bloom from March through October. Leaf color changes prolong the display through autumn, and a large greenhouse ensures plenty of bright colors even in the depths of winter.

The gardens are open daily from 9:00 a.m. to 11:00 p.m. in July and August (with spectacular lighting at night and fireworks on Saturday nights); 9:00 a.m. to 9:00 p.m. in June and September; 9:00 a.m. to 5:00 p.m. in March, April, May, and October; 9:00 a.m. to 8:00 p.m. in December; and 9:00 a.m. to 4:00 p.m. the rest of the year.

Admission is $10.17 for adults, $5.35 for students ages
13 to 17, and $1.07 for children ages 5 to 12.

(Pedestrians visiting Victoria on the ferry from Port
Angeles, Washington, can reach Butchart Gardens from
downtown on municipal bus #74.)

▲▲▲**Royal British Columbia Museum**—Besides a collection of Northwest Coast Indian artifacts only barely sur-
passed by that of the UBC Museum of Anthropology (see
tomorrow's Sightseeing Highlights), and dioramas and
multimedia displays revealing the Indians' myths and traditional way of life, the provincial museum also features
elaborate natural history exhibits showing the flora and
fauna of the seacoast, the river delta, and the coastal rain
forest. Historical re-creations let you walk backward
through time, decade by decade, experiencing sights,
sounds, and smells from the 1920s to Captain George
Vancouver's first landing on the island in 1792. This outstanding museum is located downtown at 675 Belleville
Street, next door to the Parliament buildings. It is open
daily from 9:30 a.m. to 7:00 p.m. May through August,
10:00 a.m. to 5:30 p.m. the rest of the year. Admission is
$5 for adults, $3 for senior citizens and students ages 13
to 18, and $2 for children ages 6 to 12, with a maximum
family rate of $10.

Thunderbird Park, adjoining the museum, features a
collection of totem poles, most of which depict the thunderbird, the native people's symbol for the overwhelming
power of nature. Here is your opportunity to photograph
Victoria's unique character: Indian totem poles in the fore-
ground and the Old World, elegant Empress Hotel in the
background.

Also in Thunderbird Park is the **Helmcken House**,
one of British Columbia's first pioneer homes, built in
1852 by a Hudson's Bay Company doctor. Displays include
original furnishings and medical equipment. The house is
open mid-June to mid-December daily from 10:00 a.m. to
5:00 p.m.; in September, Thursday through Monday from
10:00 a.m. to 5:00 p.m. Closed off-season. Admission is
$3 for adults, $2.25 for students, $1.25 for children ages
6 to 11.

▲**Parliament**—Intricate hand-carved facades, fountains, and statuary grace the exterior, which is illuminated after dark by more than three thousand lights. Inside, you'll find murals, wood carvings, stained-glass windows, rotundas, and British Columbian legislators. This Parliament operates by the same rules and ceremonies as Great Britain's House of Commons (there is no House of Lords, since Canada has no titled aristocracy), and it's worth watching from the galleries during sessions. Guided tours are available on weekdays and summer weekends. Call 387-3046 for the current tour schedule. Or just wander in on your own between 9:00 a.m. and 5:00 p.m. on a weekday and marvel at the architecture. The Parliament buildings were constructed entirely of British Columbian materials—except for the copper used in the domes. Today, copper is one of the province's major natural resources, but it hadn't been discovered when the Parliament buildings were unveiled in 1897 to commemorate the sixtieth year of the British queen's reign.

▲▲**Empress Hotel**—Even if you aren't planning to spend the night here (rooms start at over $150 a night during the summer months), be sure to take a look at this magnificent hotel, which has been Victoria's most recognizable landmark since it opened in 1908. The greatest accomplishment of architect Francis Rattenbury, who also designed the Parliament buildings, the Empress has hosted the rich and famous from Rudyard Kipling to John Wayne. Newly renovated in 1989, this twentieth-century castle is as elegant as hotels get. The Empress is across Belleville Street from the Royal British Columbia Museum and Thunderbird Park.

In the hotel basement is one of Victoria's most unusual commercial tourist attractions, Miniature World. For the past 25 years, circus performers Don and Honey Ray have collected miniatures from all over the world to assemble this fantastic "Greatest Little Show on Earth." Sixty exhibits include a complete, animated miniature circus, the world's largest miniature electric train layout, the world's smallest operating sawmill, two of the world's largest doll houses, the world of Charles Dickens, and a battle between ani-

mated toy soldiers. Miniature World is open daily from
8:30 a.m. to 10:00 p.m. May through October, 9:00 a.m.
to 5:30 p.m. the rest of the year. Admission is $6 for
adults, $5 for students ages 12 to 17, and $4 for children
ages 5 to 11.

▲**Maritime Museum of British Columbia**—Five blocks
north on Government Street from the Empress Hotel, at
28 Bastion Square, the Maritime Museum is packed with
sailors' gear, nautical tools, figureheads, and model ships.
The item most likely to capture your imagination is the
Tilikum, a 36-foot-long Northwest Coast Indian dugout
canoe fitted with sails, which sailed around the world
from Victoria to England in 1901-1904. The museum is
open daily from 9:00 a.m. to 8:30 p.m. during July and
August, 9:30 a.m. to 4:30 p.m. the rest of the year.
Admission is $5 for adults, $3 for senior citizens, $1
for children ages 6 to 18.

▲**Craigdarroch Castle**—Robert Dunsmuir, a Scottish
immigrant who built railroads, owned coal mines, and
eventually became the richest man on Vancouver Island,
lured his wife away from Scotland with a promise to build
her a castle grander than any in the old country. This is it.
Dunsmuir died before the castle was completed in 1889,
but his wife lived there for 19 years. Since then, it has
served as a World War I veterans' convalescent home, a
college, and a conservatory of music. In 1979, the castle
was restored as a museum. It contains period furniture,
artwork, and decor, including many of Dunsmuir's original
furnishings, and features changing exhibits on Victorian
life-styles. The castle is at 1050 Joan Crescent, 1 mile east
of the harbor via Fort Street. It is open daily from 9:00
a.m. to 9:00 p.m. mid-June through August, 9:00 a.m. to
7:00 p.m. the rest of the year. Admission is $4 for adults,
$3 for students ages 12 to 17 and senior citizens, by dona-
tion for children under 12.

Nightlife
Rock 'n' roll is scarce in this sedate, dignified city, so plan
an English traditional evening instead. Discover the fun of
an evening at the pub.

The **Pig & Whistle**, next to the Empress Hotel at 634
Humboldt Street, is a little on the touristy side (the doorman dresses like a British bobbie) but lively with music
hall acts and sing-alongs. For a more authentic pub experience, seek out **Spinnaker's** at 308 Catherine Street,
across the Johnson Street Bridge off Esquimalt Road,
where the beer is homemade and the crowd is a curious
mix of local yuppies and crusty old waterfront characters.

The top venue in Victoria for contemporary dance
music is **Harpo's** on Bastion Square near the waterfront
and the Maritime Museum. Call 385-5333 for current play-
bill and cover charge information. Or get into the old-
fashioned spirit with an evening of ballroom dancing in
the conservatory at **Crystal Gardens**.

Victoria also has a few low-key gaming casinos. (See
tomorrow's Vancouver Nightlife section for more on
British Columbia's new, limited gambling laws.) You'll
find one, the **Casino Victoria**, downtown at 716 Courtney
Street. Don't expect Las Vegas-style glitz and clatter, or
you'll be disappointed. Dress up, take your place at the
roulette table, and pretend you're James Bond.

VANCOUVER

Back on the mainland at last! In western Canada's largest city, explore a big and busy Chinese district, enjoy the view from an overhead train or a bus that runs on water, and study the world's best collection of Northwest Coast Indian artifacts.

Suggested Schedule

8:00 a.m.	Leave Victoria for Swartz Bay.
9:00 a.m.	Board the ferry for Tsawwassen.
10:35 a.m.	Arrive at Tsawwassen. Drive to downtown Vancouver.
11:15 a.m.	Park at Canada Place.
11:30 a.m.	Take a round-trip orientation ride on the Sky Train.
12:30 p.m.	Walk around Gastown and Chinatown, stopping for lunch along the way.
2:30 p.m.	Check into your accommodations.
3:00 p.m.	Drive to University of British Columbia.
3:30 p.m.	Visit the UBC Museum of Anthropology.
5:00 p.m.	Return to your accommodations.
Evening	Dinner and nightlife.

Ferry Route: Victoria to Vancouver

BC Ferries runs ferry service from Swartz Bay, on Highway 17 about 3 miles north of Sidney, where you disembarked from the San Juan Islands ferry yesterday, to Tsawwassen south of Vancouver. The ferries depart on the hour. There are always ferries at 7:00 a.m., 9:00 a.m., 11:00 a.m., 1:00 p.m., 3:00 p.m., 5:00 p.m., 7:00 p.m., and 9:00 p.m. Additional ferries leave on even-numbered hours certain days, varying seasonally. For the current ferry schedule, call 656-0757 in Victoria. The fare is $20.50 (Canadian currency only) for a car and driver, $25.50 if you're driving a motor home, and more if your vehicle is over 20 feet long or if you are towing a travel trailer. The fare for adult passengers is $4.50. Sailing time from Swartz Bay to Tsawwassen is 1 hour and 35 minutes.

Travel Route: Tsawwassen (or U.S. Border) to Downtown Vancouver

Arriving by ferry from Swartz Bay on Vancouver Island, you'll reach the mainland at Tsawwassen, about 20 miles south of downtown. From there, Highway 17 takes you to Highway 99, the main north-south freeway leading to downtown Vancouver.

If you are coming into Canada by car from the U.S. border, Interstate 5 becomes Highway 99 as it enters Canada and points you straight toward downtown Vancouver.

Either way, after crossing under the South Arm of the Fraser River via the George Massey Tunnel and over the North Arm via the Oak Street Bridge, Highway 99 becomes a congested city street. Turn west (left) to Granville Street, then north (right). Granville leads you into the heart of downtown and ends at Canada Place.

Vancouver

The province of British Columbia, spanning western Canada from the Pacific Ocean to the Rocky Mountains, is larger in area than Washington, Oregon, and California combined. Yet three-fourths of British Columbia's population lives in Vancouver and its suburbs. In sharp contrast to Victoria's British ambience, Vancouver feels thoroughly international. Only 40 percent of the city's residents are of English descent. Besides its large Chinese population (see Sightseeing Highlights), major ethnic groups in Vancouver include Italian, Greek, Japanese, Sikh, and Pakistani.

Younger than Seattle, Portland, or Victoria, the city of Vancouver was founded in 1886 when Canada's transcontinental railroad reached the Pacific Coast. Though the entire town burned to the ground just two months later, it was quickly rebuilt and within five years became the major shipping port linking Canada with Asia. In 1915, when the opening of the Panama Canal made it practical to ship lumber from the West Coast to Europe, Vancouver's

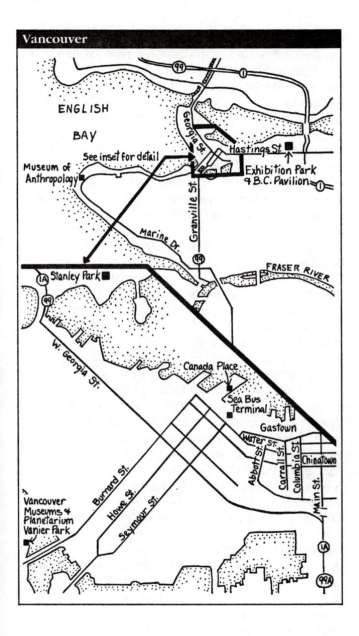

economy boomed, and the city grew larger than Seattle and Portland combined. Today, forest products remain the leading industry, and Vancouver is still the largest city in the Pacific Northwest and the third largest in Canada.

One main reason most British Columbians live in the greater Vancouver area is that the climate there is much milder than in the rest of this subarctic province. Winter temperatures in Vancouver rarely drop much below freezing. However, it is very wet, with an average annual rainfall of 57 inches—nearly twice as much as Seattle. Seventy-five percent of the days are sunless. The sun *does* come out on at least half the days in July, August, and September, and when that happens, Vancouverites seem to drop everything and take to the streets, parks, and beaches in droves. But even if your visit to Vancouver falls on a dreary, drizzly day, arm yourself with an umbrella and explore the heart of the city on foot. Sogginess is an essential element of any authentic Pacific Northwest adventure.

While satellite cities in the greater Vancouver area— West Vancouver, Coquitlam, Westminster, Langley, Delta, and Richmond—sprawl across four peninsulas and several islands linked by commuter ferries, bridges, and one of the most confusing freeway systems ever built, the city of Vancouver itself nestles on a single arm of land bounded by Burrard Inlet on the north and the north arm of the Fraser River on the south. Downtown Vancouver, including Canada Place, Gastown, Chinatown, and Stanley Park, is on a spit of land jutting into Burrard Inlet midway along the north side of the peninsula. The University of British Columbia is on the western tip of the peninsula.

Sightseeing Highlights
▲▲**Canada Place**—Like Seattle, Vancouver has hosted a World's Fair. Unlike Seattle Center, though, Vancouver's fairgrounds from 1986 have not been preserved intact. Much of the main fair site has been rebuilt as offices and public housing. The huge Canada Pavilion remains on the waterfront near the end of Granville Street. Now called Canada Place, it features a 17-story geodesic sphere and

five 80-foot-tall fiberglass "sails" designed to suggest a clipper ship in the harbor. Primarily a trade center and convention complex with an expensive hotel and restaurant, as well as a cruise ship terminal, Canada Place also has international fast-food places, an exhibit of totem poles and native quilts, and an Imax theater with showings hourly from 12:00 noon to 10:00 p.m. Admission is $6 daytime/$7 at night for adults, $5/$7 for senior citizens and students, and $3.50/$5.50 for children. Call 682-IMAX for current show information.

You can learn about Vancouver's history from dozens of information plaques along the outdoor Promenade Into History around Canada Place. Guide yourself or take one of the free tours that depart frequently from the information booth on the downtown side of Canada Place.

▲▲**The Sky Train and the Sea Bus**—The computer-operated, magnetically driven, elevated Sky Train starts from the station two blocks east of Canada Place on Cordova Street and runs 16 miles east to suburban Burnaby, Westminster, and Surrey. A round trip is a great way to get an overview of the greater Vancouver area. You don't need to ride the whole route (the fare is higher if you go beyond the Vancouver city limits); just hop off at any station and catch the next train back. Sky trains run every five minutes from 5:30 a.m. to 1:00 a.m.

The Sea Bus passenger ferry starts at its terminal just across Canada Place from the Sky Train station and runs across Burrard Inlet to North Vancouver, providing a fine view of the waterfront. It operates weekdays from 6:15 a.m. to 1:00 a.m., Saturdays from 6:30 a.m. to 1:00 a.m., and Sundays from 8:30 a.m. to 11:30 p.m. Departures are every 15 minutes from 6:15 a.m. to 7:15 p.m. weekdays and 10:15 a.m. to 7:15 p.m. Saturdays, every half hour the rest of the time.

One-way fares on both the Sky Train and the Sea Bus are $1.25 for adults, 65 cents for children ages 5 to 13 and seniors 65 and older. (It costs 50 cents more to ride the Sky Train to New Westminster or $1.25 more to ride all the way to Surrey.) Fares are higher during rush hours. You can buy a one-day unlimited travel pass valid on both the Sky Train and the Sea Bus as well as municipal buses for $3.50, a money-saver if you want to ride both the train and the ferry. Exact change, Canadian money only, is required.

Beatles Museum—Remember them? If you do, you might want to walk five blocks down Seymour Street from the Sky Train station to RPM Records. The "museum," actually a large memorabilia shop offering just about everything a die-hard Beatlemaniac could conceivably long for, is upstairs. Hours are Tuesday through Sunday from 12:00 noon to 5:00 p.m., until 6:00 p.m. on Saturdays.

▲▲**Gastown**—Nineteen years before Vancouver was founded, a colorful pioneer entrepreneur by the name of John "Gassy Jack" Deighton opened the area's first saloon, catering to lumberjacks from nearby logging camps and sawmills, on the site that is now Maple Tree Square—the intersection of Carrall, Powell, Walter, and Alexander streets, six blocks southeast of Granville Street and Canada Place. The story of Gassy Jack is a dismal one: the saloon owner married a twelve-year-old girl, was cuckolded, raised a son who was not his own as his only heir, lived to see his bar and the neighborhood around it destroyed by fire in 1896, and drank himself to death. Always the "bad part of town," Gastown declined during the Great Depression to become perhaps the most decrepit and disreputable waterfront slum on the West Coast.

Refurbishment of this historic district began in the 1960s, and today Gastown is Vancouver's showpiece historic district, packed with galleries, boutiques, craft shops, night clubs, and restaurants, all aimed at the tourist trade. A big bronze statue of Gassy Jack, posthumously vindicated as a man of foresight and a local hero, stands atop a bronze whiskey barrel in Maple Tree Square. Nearby, at the corner of Cambie and Water streets, North America's only steam-powered clock chimes every 15 minutes. Walk around and explore the district's notorious past and artsy-cutesy present in side passageways with names like Gaoler's Mews and Blood Alley.

▲▲**Chinatown**—One-fourth of Vancouver's population is of Chinese descent, and this minority group is growing as tens of thousands of people from Hong Kong buy property in Vancouver each year to gain landed immigrant status and a new home in Canada before Hong Kong becomes part of the People's Republic of China in 1997. Already, Vancouver's Chinese-American community rivals San Francisco's in numbers. With immigration from Hong Kong, it is expected to become the largest in the Western Hemisphere any day now. Vancouver's Chinatown is less tourist-oriented than San Francisco's, but you'll find plenty of shops offering gift items of jade and silk, as well as other shops and sidewalk market stalls displaying exotic vegetables, mysterious-looking herbs and elixirs, and smoked ducks hung by their heels. It's enough to make you forget which side of the Pacific you're on.

The heart of Chinatown is within walking distance of Gastown. From Maple Tree Square, follow Carrall Street south to Pender Street. At the intersection, the Chinese Cultural Center shows free changing exhibits on local history and culture and has a bookstore where you can buy a detailed walking tour map of Chinatown. Pender Street east of Carrall is Chinatown's main business street.

Dr. Sun Yat-sen Park and Classical Chinese Garden is a block south of the cultural center on Carrall. The $6 million garden is patterned after gardens in the Chinese city of Suzhou that date back to the Ming dynasty (fourteenth to seventeenth centuries). Most of its architectural elements are antiques brought from China. The garden is open daily from 10:00 a.m. to 7:30 p.m. Admission is $3.50 for adults, $2.50 for children ages 6 to 11 and seniors over 65, maximum $7 for families.

▲**Stanley Park**—This 1,000-acre park, just a 15-minute walk or a 5-minute drive north of downtown Vancouver via Georgia Street, is one of the finest natural city parks in North America. Much of Stanley Park is wooded with fir and cedar, providing a home for abundant wildlife within sight of the city skyscrapers. You can walk for miles along forest trails, beaches, or the seawall promenade. Within the park are the Vancouver Zoo (open during daylight hours, admission $1.90 per adult, 90 cents for children under age 13 and senior citizens) and the excellent

Vancouver Aquarium (open 9:30 a.m. to 8:00 p.m. during
the summer, 10:00 a.m. to 5:00 p.m. the rest of the year,
admission $8 per adult, $7 for students ages 13 to 18 and
senior citizens, $5 for children ages 5 to 12). Other facili-
ties in Stanley Park include cricket fields, lawn bowling
greens, a golf course, tennis courts, a rose garden, a totem
pole display, and an open-air theater.

▲**H. R. MacMillan Planetarium and Vancouver
Museum**—One of the largest and best-equipped planetari-
ums in North America, H. R. MacMillan boasts a $1 million
Zeiss star projector and hundreds of computer-controlled
special effects projectors as well as a sophisticated laser
imaging system. Astronomy shows are presented during
July and August daily at 1:00, 2:30, 4:00, and 7:00 p.m., the
rest of the year Tuesday through Sunday at 2:30 and 7:00
p.m., with additional shows at 1:00 p.m. on Friday and 1:00
and 4:00 p.m. on Saturday and Sunday, closed Mondays
September through June. The most spectacular special
effects can be seen in the planetarium's laser light shows
with rock music sound tracks (Pink Floyd shows have been
a perennial favorite here for more than 15 years), presented
Tuesday through Sunday at 8:30 p.m. as well as Friday and
Saturday at 9:45 p.m. Admission to the astronomy shows is
$4.75 for adults and $3.25 for children under age 17 and
senior citizens, with a $12 maximum family rate; admission
to laser shows is $6.50 for everybody.

The planetarium is in the same cone-shaped building as
the Vancouver Museum which contains dioramas of nineteenth-century life in British Columbia, including replicas
of a pioneer trading post, an Edwardian home, and a railroad car. Other features are natural history exhibits and
Northwest Coast Indian artifacts. The museum is open
from 10:00 a.m. to 9:00 p.m. daily during July and August,
10:00 a.m. to 5:00 p.m. Tuesday through Sunday the rest
of the year. Admission is $5 per adult, $2.50 for children
ages 6 to 18 and senior citizens, with a $10 maximum
family rate.

The planetarium and museum are situated in Vanier
Park overlooking Sunset Beach. To get there, take Burrard

Street (two blocks west of Granville) south from down-town. Vanier Park is just over the Burrard Bridge.

▲**Exhibition Park**—The attraction that makes this public park worth the drive is a giant relief map—76 feet by 80 feet—of the entire province of British Columbia. It is located in the B.C. Pavilion, which also houses the British Columbia Sports Hall of Fame. The pavilion is open Monday through Friday, 9:15 a.m. to 4:45 p.m., closed weekends and holidays. Admission is free. Also in Exhibition Park is Playland Amusement Park, a traditional amusement park featuring the biggest wooden roller coaster in Canada. Call 255-5161 for current hours. An all-day ride pass costs $12.95 if you're under 4 feet tall, otherwise $16.95. Exhibition Park is several miles east of downtown via East Hastings Street, between Renfrew and Cassiar streets.

▲▲▲**UBC Museum of Anthropology**—Here is your best opportunity to learn more about the Haida, Kwakiutl, Tsimshian, and other native peoples of British Columbia's coast whose totem designs are seen everywhere in the Pacific Northwest. They wove their stylized bird and animal motifs into tapestries and hats, painted them on house facades, and carved them on poles, masks, canoe prows, and ceremonial bowls. The Northwest Coast Indians based their economy on gift giving (and the obligation to recipro-cate), which not only built a sophisticated system for dis-tributing resources but also created a need for all sorts of decorative items. Contact with European whalers, mer-chants, and colonists, who based their business dealings on something other than generosity, destroyed the native way of life in an ironic way: as villages grew prosperous through trade, they held more and more lavish potlatches (gift-giving feasts) that bankrupted many. Foreign diseases killed more than 90 percent of the Northwest Coast Indians by the early twentieth century. Today, the only remaining native people on the British Columbia coast who live in the traditional ways are the Haida, who sparsely inhabit the remote Queen Charlotte Islands, only accessible by ferry from the port of Prince Rupert, about 300 miles northwest of Vancouver. It's 850 miles by the shortest road.

The Museum of Anthropology at the University of British Columbia houses the world's finest collection of Northwest Coast Indian artifacts, from a replica Haida village and a large totem pole collection to hundreds of pull-out display drawers full of jewelry, pipes, fetishes, and other small objects. There are also contemporary Northwest Coast Indian wood sculptures as well as international archaeology exhibits.

The museum is located at 6393 NW Marine Drive. To get there from Granville Street, just south of the Granville Bridge turn west onto 47th Avenue and go about 4 miles. Turn left onto NW Marine Drive, which curves around through the UBC campus. The museum is near the tip of the peninsula. It is open Tuesday from 11:00 a.m. to 9:00 p.m. and Wednesday through Sunday from 11:00 a.m. to 5:00 p.m. Admission is $5 for adults, $2.50 for students and senior citizens, and free for children under age 6. On Tuesdays, admission is free. You can also reach the university from downtown by taking municipal bus #10; return on bus #14. Bus fares are the same as those for the Sky Train and Sea Bus (see above) and are covered by the same daily pass.

Near the Museum of Anthropology is a half-mile trail that descends very steeply down the Point Grey cliffs to Wreck Beach. The cliff climb puts this beach beyond the reach of law enforcement and Anglo-Canadian prudery. It is Vancouver's only nude beach, popular on those rare days when the sun shines. The trail can be hazardous in the rain.

Camping

There are no public campgrounds in the greater Vancouver area. The closest is at **Porteau Cove Provincial Park**, about 21 miles north of the city via Highway 99, with a swimming beach but no hookups. To get the most out of a visit to the city, even confirmed campers should consider taking a downtown hotel room tonight. For those who wish to see Vancouver as a day trip, the **Park Canada Recreational Vehicle Inn**, about 2 miles east of the ferry terminal at Tsawwassen, offers full hookups and amenities for $18 a night. If you're entering Canada via Interstate 5/Highway 99, the **KOA Vancouver**, 8 miles north of the border crossing, charges $16.50 a night.

Lodging

The grandest old hotel in downtown Vancouver is the **Hotel Vancouver** at 900 West Georgia Street, (604) 684-3131 or toll-free (800) 828-7447 from the United States and (800) 268-9411 from Canada. King George VI of England stayed here shortly after the hotel opened in 1939, and as a guest today you'll feel like royalty too. Edwardian elegance pervades the hotel lobby with its marble columns and crystal chandeliers; the rooms are modern, quiet, and spacious. Room rates are steep, ranging from about $185 to $300 Canadian from April through October, about $50 less during the winter months, with lavish suites running as much as $1,250 a night. Even so, you'd pay more at several of the contemporary luxury hotels downtown.

A more moderately priced classic hotel downtown is the art deco-style **Abbotsford Hotel** at 921 West Pender Street, (604) 681-4335 or toll-free (800) 663-1700. Room rates are about $80 a night during tourist season, $50 during the winter months.

One of Vancouver's nicest small bed and breakfasts is the **Johnson House**, located at 34th and Vine streets in the Kerrisdale district, a residential neighborhood out toward the University of British Columbia. This antique-filled home features a lovely rock garden and decor accented by wooden carousel animals. Rates range from $50 to $90 a night. For reservations, call (604) 266-4175.

Look in Gastown for low-priced lodging. The turn-of-the-century **Dominion Hotel** at the corner of Abbot and Water streets, (604) 681-6666, offers clean, simple rooms and a lobby full of Victorian antiques at around $50 a night; the only drawback is that there is no elevator, so you reach your room by climbing the kind of giant staircase they don't make any more. Spartan rooms, budget-priced, can be found at the **Niagara Hotel**, 435 West Pender Street, (604) 688-7574, where doubles run $30 to $40 a night. In the same price range, downtown but not in

Gastown, are the **YMCA**, 955 Burrard Street, (604) 681-0221, open to both men and women, and the **YWCA**, 580 Burrard Street, (604) 662-8188, for women, couples, and families but not single men; both offer private rooms with shared baths.

Dormitory accommodations cost as little as $8 per person at the **Vancouver Hostel** (IYH), Canada's largest youth hostel, south of downtown at 1515 Discovery Street, (604) 224-3208, closed 10:00 a.m. to 4:00 p.m., and the **Backpackers Youth Hostel** (unaffiliated) near Chinatown at 929 Main Street, (604) 682-2441, no closed hours or curfew.

Food

Situated under the sails at Canada Place, **The Prow** is a contemporary Vancouver landmark where you can dine with a view of Burrard Inlet or the cruise ship terminal. The cuisine is expensive and extraordinary, with a focus on fresh fish and seafood. The Prow is open daily from 11:30 a.m. to 2:00 p.m. for lunch and 5:30 to 10:30 p.m. for dinner. For reservations, call 684-1339.

Among the dozens of restaurants in Chinatown, two good bets are the **On On Tea Garden** at 214 Keefer Street, open Tuesday through Thursday from 11:00 a.m. to 9:00 p.m., Friday and Saturday from 11:00 a.m. to 10:00 p.m., and Sunday from 4:00 to 10:00 p.m., 685-7513; and the **New Diamond Restaurant** at 555 Gore Avenue between Pender and Keefer, open daily except Wednesdays from 7:30 a.m. to 3:00 p.m. and 5:00 to 10:00 p.m., 685-0727. You can also dine affordably and well from sidewalk vendors' dim sum carts along the main streets of Chinatown.

Noodle Makers, one of the best Chinese restaurants around, is not in Chinatown but in neighboring Gastown at 122 Powell Street. Inside, you'll find traditional decor, including nineteenth-century Chinese-American antiques, as well as a goldfish pool and a waterfall. Entrées, each served on a bed of fresh handmade noodles, include imaginative salmon, crab, oyster, and shrimp dishes.

Prices are moderate. The restaurant is open for lunch on weekdays only from 11:30 a.m. to 2:00 p.m. and for dinner nightly from 5:00 to 10:00 p.m. For reservations, call 253-4316.

You can find a truly international mix of restaurants in Gastown. Consider **India Village** (East Indian) at 308 Water Street, open daily from 11:00 a.m. to 11:00 p.m., 681-0678; **Phnom Penh Restaurant** (Cambodian) at 244 East Georgia Street, open daily except Tuesday from 11:00 a.m. to 11:00 p.m., 682-5777; **Le Railcar** (French) at 106 Carrall, open for lunch on weekdays only from 11:30 a.m. to 2:00 p.m. and for dinner nightly (closed Sundays off-season) from 5:30 to 10:00 p.m., 669-5422; **Kilimanjaro** (East African) at 322 Water Street, open for lunch on weekdays only from 11:30 a.m. to 4:00 p.m. and for dinner daily from 5:30 to 11:00 p.m., 681-9913; or **Al Forno** (Italian—great pizzas!) at Columbia and Water streets, open for lunch Sunday and Tuesday through Friday from 11:30 a.m. to 2:00 p.m. and for dinner Sunday and Tuesday through Thursday from 5:00 to 11:00 p.m., Friday and Saturday from 5:00 p.m. to 12:30 a.m., 684-2838.

Nightlife

Vancouver is a good city for live theater. Most nights there are about a dozen plays in performance, ranging from repertory standards and touring company productions of recent Broadway hits to works by Canada's best contemporary playwrights. Check the daily papers or the weekly Georgia Straight arts and entertainment publication for current playbills. The most offbeat of Vancouver stage venues is the improvisational **Back Alley Theatre** at Georgia and Thurlow streets, 688-7013.

Gastown is a good place for nightclub hopping. Look for jazz in an Irish pub atmosphere at the **Blarney Stone**, 216 Carrall Street, 687-4322; disco at **Amnesia**, 99 Powell Street, 682-2211; or rock at the **Town Pump**, 66 Water Street, 683-6695.

Casino gambling is legal in Vancouver, with certain restrictions. Casinos are limited in size to 15 tables, craps and other dice games are prohibited, and the maximum bet is $5. Perhaps the most intriguing gambling house in town, because of its multicultural clientele, is the **Vancouver Casino** on the edge of Chinatown at Main and East Georgia streets, 253-4263. Alongside the roulette and blackjack tables you'll find the Chinese favorite, *sicbo*.

NORTH CASCADES HIGHWAY

The North Cascades Highway is said by many to be the most scenic route in Washington, and on a busy summer weekend you may find a paradox there: bumper-to-bumper seekers of wilderness solitude. Much of the time, though—especially on weekdays—heavy traffic is not a problem. The highway runs through Ross Lake National Recreation Area, a narrow strip that divides the two halves of North Cascades National Park. The national park itself is entirely wilderness area, accessible only on foot or horseback. The same National Park Service office that administers North Cascades National Park also administers Ross Lake National Recreation Area, as well as Lake Chelan National Recreation Area (Day 9), so in effect all three areas form a single national park.

Suggested Schedule

7:30 a.m.	Breakfast and leave Vancouver.
8:30 a.m.	Cross the border into the United States.
9:30 a.m.	Drive the North Cascades Highway to Mazama.
12:00 noon	Stop for a picnic lunch at Rainy Pass.
1:00 p.m.	Drive to Mazama.
1:30 p.m.	Drive up Hart's Pass Road.
2:00 p.m.	Hike the Pacific Crest Trail (part of it, anyway).
3:00 p.m.	Return to Mazama. Drive on to Chelan.
5:00 p.m.	Arrive in Chelan, camp or check into your motel.
6:00 p.m.	Dinner.

Note for Off-Season Travelers

Days 8 through 10 of this itinerary are not usable during the late fall, winter, and early spring. The North Cascades Highway is closed until early May. The Lake Chelan cruise (Day 9) operates on a limited schedule year-round, but from November through April you can only get to Chelan from the west side of the mountains via the Stevens Pass Highway, US 2 east, which exits I-5 at Everett. The back way into Mount Rainier National Park (Day 10) is also closed in winter, though the park itself is open to Paradise and can be reached from Seattle or Tacoma in less than two hours' drive.

Travel Route: Vancouver to Chelan (269 miles)

From downtown Vancouver, go south across the Granville Bridge and follow Highway 99 south. Drive 31 miles and you'll reach the border, where you clear U.S. Customs and the highway becomes Interstate 5. Continue south for 49 miles, passing through the small city of Bellingham, and exit east on Highway 20. Take Highway 20 through Sedro Wooley, Lyman, and Concrete, where a road turns off to the north for Mount Baker Recreation Area, a winter sports area. This morning's route takes you through a portion of Mount Baker-Snoqualmie National Forest, which extends down the west side of the Cascade Range from the border to Mount Rainier. Mount Baker (10,778 feet) has been showing signs of volcanic activity since 1975, and some experts believe it will be the next Cascades volcano to blow its top—but probably not today. Recently, Mount Baker-Snoqualmie National Forest has seen disturbances of a different sort as the epicenter of the Northern Spotted Owl War between conservationists and the forest products industry. Your chances of actually seeing one of these elusive, nocturnal birds are only slightly better than your chances of spotting a Sasquatch (bigfoot), but on today's drive you will see in the distance vast expanses of coniferous forests, some of which have never been touched by lumberjacks. And you'll have an opportunity to ponder (not for the last time on this 22-day trip) why it is that we Americans are cutting the last stands of ancient trees in our national forests at a faster percentage rate than Brazilians are clearing the Amazon rain forest, exporting one-third of the logs to Japan, and recycling less of our waste paper than Japan and most Asian, Latin American, and European nations do. Remember, the forests you'll see on today's trip belong to you.

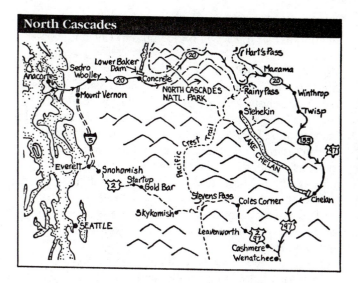

North Cascades

Continue on Highway 20 past the lower dam of Baker Lake, through Rockport, Marblemount, and Newhalem to Ross Lake. It is 67 miles from I-5 to Newhalem, the last town before the high mountains.

In the North Cascades, you will not find the visitor amenities or commercial concessions that characterize many U.S. national parks. In fact, beyond Newhalem you won't find gas, food, or lodging for 75 miles. What you will find is some of the most spectacular mountain scenery in the United States.

Thirty miles beyond Newhalem, you'll crest Rainy Pass. Here and at Washington Pass, 5 miles farther, overlooks afford spectacular views of the rugged North Cascades to the north, south, and west. A segment of the Pacific Crest Trail parallels the road for about a mile near Rainy Pass, where you can hike if the Hart's Pass Road is closed by snow or sounds too ambitious. From Washington Pass, it's 17 miles to Mazama, where you turn off to reach Hart's Pass.

After your Pacific Crest hike, continue on Highway 20 for 27 miles, through the towns of Winthrop and Twisp. About three miles past Twisp, Highway 153 forks off to the right. Follow Highway 153 south to the junction with

US 97, a distance of 31 miles. Turn right (south) on US 97, and another 17 miles will bring you into Chelan.

Sightseeing Highlight

▲▲**The Pacific Crest Trail**—The United States' longest and most famous National Scenic Trail runs all the way from the Canadian border to the Mexican border along the Cascade and Sierra Nevada mountain ranges. You will intersect it three more times later in this tour: at Cascade Locks where it crosses the Columbia River; on the south slope of Mount Hood; and in Crater Lake National Park. To hike the whole Pacific Crest Trail takes several months, but you can try a tiny sample of the experience and imagine the rest on a short detour from the North Cascades Highway. Here's how.

One mile beyond the Early Winters Forest Service Information Station, turn off the highway into Mazama, then turn right on Hart's Pass Road. (Snow closes this unpaved road in the winter, sometimes until mid-June, and trailers are not allowed past Ballard Campground.) The road twists and climbs switchbacks for 13 miles from Mazama to the 6,197-foot crest of the North Cascades. Just beyond Meadows Campground, you can hike on the Pacific Crest Trail as far as you want in either direction from the trailhead.

Afterward, return to the main highway the same way you came.

Camping

Chelan has a big municipal campground—essentially a city-run RV park—right in the middle of town, with showers and a lakefront beach. The camping fee is $11. Except for a handful of unappealing tent sites, the campground is for RVs only.

A more pleasant lakeside campground is at **Lake Chelan State Park**, 4 miles west of town on US 97 and then 5 miles northwest on Shore Drive. Standard sites cost $8, with a few higher-priced sites that have hookups. The only drawback to this campground is that the distance from town means you'll have to rise and shine earlier to break camp and be at the boat dock for the 8:30 a.m. departure tomorrow morning. Campground reservations are required at Lake Chelan State Park between Memorial Day and Labor Day. Request a reservation form from the Washington State Parks and Recreation Commission, 7150 Clearwater Lane, KY-ll, Olympia, WA 98504, (206) 753-2027. (See Day 4, Camping, for more information on reservation procedures.) The reservation address for Lake Chelan State Park is Route 1, Box 90, Chelan, WA 98816.

Lodging

Chelan has plenty of motels, none of them low priced: the going rates are $45 to $70. With luck, budget travelers may be able to land one of the few $49 rooms (as low as $30 off-season) at the **Apple Inn Motel**, 1002 East Woodin, (509) 682-4044, which has an outdoor swimming pool and a year-round hot tub.

Campbell's Resort, the town's historic lakefront lodge (circa 1901) at 104 West Woodin, (509) 682-2561, has main lodge rooms, modern motel-style units, and private cabins. In 1991, the resort is opening a new 40-unit complex to replace some of the housekeeping cabins. Amenities include a beach, a whirlpool spa, and three swimming pools. Rates start at $114 a night during July and August but gradually drop to about half that during the off-season (November to May).

Mary Kay's Whaley Mansion, at 415 Third Street, is Chelan's showpiece B&B, a big Edwardian house festooned with "gingerbread" and packed with antiques and elaborate interior decor. Rates start at $95. Reservations are essential. Call (509) 682-5735. More affordable B&B accommodations can be found at **Em's Bed & Breakfast Inn**, 304 E. Wapato, (509) 682-4149, about $60.

Condominium resorts and private owners frequently rent units by the night (sometimes requiring three-night minimum stays) for about twice the price of an ordinary motel room. Kitchen facilities make them a reasonable alternative for several people traveling together. Contact

the Lake Chelan Chamber of Commerce, P.O. Box 216,
Chelan, WA 98816, (800) 4CHELAN, for current condominium rental information.

Food
The **Campbell House** restaurant in Campbell's Resort
lives up to its long-standing reputation as Chelan's finest
restaurant. Dinners start at about $10. For reservations, call
682-4250.

Chelan has other restaurants in abundance, mostly pre-
dictable family restaurants and fast-food places. Anywhere
in town, you won't have to search far for fried chicken,
pizza, or hamburgers.

LAKE CHELAN

Now you're on the east side of the Cascade Mountains, known as the "dry side" because the mountains catch the ocean's moisture and cast a rain shadow, which makes the eastern half of both Washington and Oregon a high desert.

I asked diligently among Seattlites, "What's there to see east of the mountains?" Usually the question brought a blank stare. "Rattlesnakes," said a graduate of Washington State University in Pullman, on the state's eastern border, who ought to know what's out there. "And wheat fields," he added, "lots of wheat fields."

Actually, there's much more to the "dry side," beginning today with an all-day cruise into the heart of the North Cascades.

Suggested Schedule

7:30 a.m.	Breakfast.
8:30 a.m.	Board the *Lady of the Lake*. Cruise up Lake Chelan.
12:30 p.m.	Arrive in Stehekin.
2:00 p.m.	Leave Stehekin.
6:00 p.m.	Arrive back in Chelan.

Lake Chelan: The *Lady of the Lake* Cruise

More than 1,500 feet deep (the lake bottom is below sea level), Lake Chelan is among the world's deepest lakes. In the United States, only Crater Lake (Day 16) is deeper. As you travel up the lake by boat, its narrowness makes it seem more like a great river: 55 miles in length, it is only about 2 miles across at its widest point and, in other places, only half a mile across. Some visitors mistakenly assume that Lake Chelan is man-made; certainly, it appears similar to Franklin Roosevelt Lake to the west, formed by Grand Coulee Dam, and a dam at the south end of the lake raises the water level by 21 feet. In fact, Lake Chelan is a natural phenomenon. The glacier that

gouged this deep canyon, or coulee, through the North
Cascades during the last ice age pushed ahead of it a
massive wall of mud and rocks that formed a natural
dam at the lower end of the coulee.

While the lower end of the lake is a busy resort area
where many Seattlites come to escape rainy weather, Lake
Chelan thrusts northward deep into the heart of the North
Cascades, providing a navigable waterway through the
Sawtooth and Glacier Peak wilderness areas, which are
inaccessible by road. You can glide through the wilderness, between sheer cliffs at the foot of glacier-clad peaks,
on the *Lady of the Lake*, originally a private ferry serving
small communities at the north end of Lake Chelan. Today
it is a popular excursion cruise, and the only way for
backpackers to reach the south boundary of North Cascades National Park. Mile for mile, the *Lady of the Lake*
may be the best cruise bargain in the United States. It is
undoubtedly one of the most scenic: even the San Juan
Islands ferry trip pales by comparison!

The first hour of the cruise takes you past seemingly
endless lakefront vacation cottages. Then you pass
beyond the reach of civilization, between 8,000-foot
mountains where small streams tumble as much as half
a mile down sheer cliff faces. Watch carefully with binoculars handy: you're likely to see mountain goats travers-
ing the cliffs. After a brief stop at Lucerne, the port for
Holden, a well-preserved historic mining town and wilderness trailhead, you'll arrive at noon in Stehekin, the village
at the north end of the lake. In Stehekin, you can get
information on the numerous hiking trails in the area from
the North Cascades National Park visitor center, which is
in a converted 1920s resort hotel. A few other small hotels
are still in operation, including one where you can eat
lunch. There are also some rustic private homes and a historic homestead with interpretive signs about pioneer life.
For a small fee, a shuttle bus will take you 3 miles to
Rainbow Falls. Since Stehekin cannot be reached by road,
you may be surprised at the number of old, beat-up auto-
mobiles in the village. Brought on barges, the cars take

local residents up and down the 22-mile road between the ferry dock and homesteads in the valley.

If you choose to stay longer in Stehekin, you can arrange a half-day guided horseback trip to Coon Lake ($25 per person, groups limited to 6 people), take a sightseeing flight over the North Cascades ($70 for 2 passengers), or rent a mountain bike ($3.50 per hour or $20 all day).

"Stehekin" is a Native American word meaning "the way through." For both Indians and early pioneers, a main route from inland Washington through the Cascade Mountains to the coast was to canoe up Lake Chelan and the Stehekin River, climb 5,400-foot Cascade Pass, and follow the Cascade River west. This route brought them out of the mountains at Marblemount, where you started into the mountains on the North Cascades Highway yesterday. At Stehekin, you are only about 11 miles straight-line distance from Rainy Pass on the North Cascades Highway; it would take two days to walk there.

Cruise Information

The *Lady of the Lake* leaves the Lake Chelan Boat Company dock at the south end of the lake, a short distance west of the town center on US 97, daily from April 15 through October 15, at 8:30 a.m. The *Lady of the Lake* is a different boat at different times of year—a sleek, modern 90-passenger excursion boat in the summer peak season or, at slower times of year, a comfortable, lovingly cared for older craft that carries up to two dozen passengers. Reservations are not taken. Be at the dock soon after 8:00 a.m. If the office is open, buy your tickets; otherwise, simply board the boat and a crew member will take your fare sometime during the northbound cruise. The round-trip fare for this all-day cruise is $21 per adult, half-price for children ages 6 to 11. No pets are allowed on board during the busy summer season. For more information, contact Lake Chelan Boat Company, P.O. Box 186, Chelan, WA 98816, (509) 682-4584.

For those visitors who are on a tight schedule or are easily bored by long boat trips, the Lake Chelan Boat

Company has recently added a new, faster boat, called the *Lady Express* which cuts the round-trip time from Chelan to Stehekin in half. The *Lady Express* leaves at 8:30 a.m., arrives in Stehekin at 10:30 a.m., leaves Stehekin at 11:55 a.m., and arrives back in Chelan at 1:30 p.m. The round-trip fare is $39 for adults, half-price for children ages 2 through 11. In the summer, you can ride one way on the *Lady Express* and return on the *Lady of the Lake*, allowing yourself 3½ hours in Stehekin, for $30. Off-season, the *Lady Express* makes the trip Monday, Wednesday, and Friday year-round, as well as Sundays from mid-February to mid-April.

The most spectacular way to see Lake Chelan is to take a sightseeing flight one way to Stehekin on Chelan Airways ($40 per person, reservations recommended, call 509-682-5555) and take the boat back (one-way fare is $14 per person).

Food and Lodging

Following this itinerary to the letter, you'll return to Chelan this evening and stay at the same campground or lodgings as you did last night. But if one of your vacation priorities is to "get away from it all" (and I mean all of it), consider spending the night—or a week—in Stehekin. The main accommodations are at the 26-unit **North Cascades Lodge**, which has a restaurant and small grocery store. Rates for doubles are under $50 off-season, rising to about $70 between July 1 and October 15. For information and reservations, write North Cascades Lodge, P.O. Box 275, Stehekin, WA 98852, or call (509) 682-4711. Also in Stehekin, the **Silver Bay Inn Bed and Breakfast**, Box 43, Stehekin, WA 98852, (509) 682-2212 (Monday through Friday 8:00 a.m. to 5:00 p.m.) offers a suite and guest cabins for $85 to $95 a night. Breakfast is included in the main B&B facility, while the cabins have complete kitchens including microwave and dishwasher. The Silver Bay Inn provides canoes and bikes free to guests. The **Stehekin Pastry Company**, one mile from the boat landing, sells cinnamon rolls, pies, croissants, pastries, and frozen yogurt from 7:00 a.m. to 8:00 p.m.

APPLE COUNTRY AND MOUNT RAINIER

One of the images that probably comes to mind when you think of Washington State is apples. Big, bright, red, juicy, delicious ones. This morning, you'll drive through the heart of apple-growing country. In the afternoon, you'll continue down the dry, pine-forested eastern slope of the Cascades to approach Mount Rainier by the less used "back door" route.

Today's is a fairly long drive, much of it on highways that are not particularly fast, and you'll want to arrive at Paradise on Mount Rainier before 4:00 p.m. if you plan to spend the night there. The route is scenic but leaves little time for sightseeing. According to your interests, choose between a stroll around Leavenworth and a visit to the Yakima Indian Cultural Center. For those travelers who wish to take an extra day to explore Washington's dry side, perhaps spending a night in Yakima, I've included brief information on other sightseeing highlights in the Travel Route section.

Suggested Schedule

7:30 a.m.	Breakfast.
8:30 a.m.	Drive from Chelan to Leavenworth.
10:00 a.m.	Visit Leavenworth and pick up the makings for a picnic lunch.
11:00 a.m.	Drive to Yakima, picnicking en route.
1:00 p.m.	Arrive in Yakima. (Allow an extra two hours in your schedule if you wish to visit the Yakima Indian Cultural Center in Toppenish, 15 miles to the south.) Then drive to Mount Rainier.
2:30 p.m.	Enter Mount Rainier National Park.
3:30 p.m.	Arrive at Paradise. Check into the lodge or find a campsite.
4:00 p.m.	Enjoy a late-afternoon hike on the slopes of Mount Rainier.

Travel Route: Chelan to Mount Rainier National Park (228 miles plus side trips)

US 97 is the main north-south highway along the eastern slope of the Cascades. You'll encounter this highway repeatedly from here to Crater Lake (Day 16). Take US 97 south, through desert country along the banks of the Columbia River, for 35 miles to the highway intersection on the outskirts of Wenatchee. Along the way, you'll pass Rocky Reach Dam and, 4 miles farther along, Ohme Gardens.

Rocky Reach Dam has a fish ladder with an underwater viewing area where you can watch adult salmon swim up the river to spawn and fingerlings swim down to the sea. This is a less crowded place to watch the Columbia salmon run than Bonneville Dam (Day 13). The visitor center's Gallery of Electricity traces developments from Ben Franklin's kite to microchips. Open daily from 8:00 a.m. to 8:00 p.m. Memorial Day to Labor Day, 8:00 a.m. to 5:00 p.m. the rest of the year, closed January 1 to February 15, free admission.

Ohme Gardens, a 9-acre formal garden on a rocky point overlooking the Wenatchee Valley and the Columbia River, has been landscaped using native mountain plants. Stone pathways among rugged basalt formations connect various levels of the garden, which features evergreen trees, fern grotto pools, and a wishing well. The gardens are open mid-April to mid-October, 9:00 a.m. to dusk. Admission is $5 for adults, $3 for children ages 7 to 17.

The intersection of US 97 and US 2 on the outskirts of Wenatchee is complicated. Follow the signs closely to stay on US 97 in the direction of Cashmere and Leavenworth. If you find yourself in downtown Wenatchee, you took a wrong turn. (But all is not lost—Wenatchee is the heart of Washington's apple-growing country, and the **North Central Washington Museum**, at 127 South Mission Street, can tell you everything you ever wanted to know about apples. A complete antique apple-processing factory is in a separate building connected to the main museum by a skybridge. There is also a film and an exhibit about the first trans-Pacific airplane flight, in 1931, which started

Apple Country

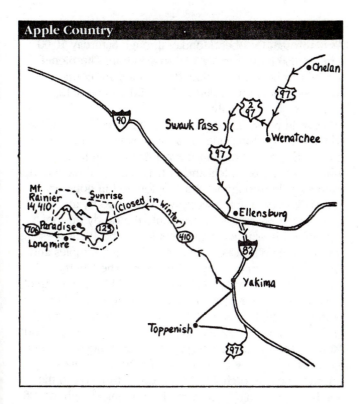

from Japan and ended, improbably, in Wenatchee. The museum is open Monday through Friday from 10:00 a.m. to 4:00 p.m., Saturday and Sunday from 1:00 p.m. to 4:00 p.m. Admission is $2 for adults, $1 for children ages 8 to 12.)

From Wenatchee, stay on US 2/97 for about 5 miles west to Cashmere, where you'll see **Chelan County Museum and Pioneer Village** on your left. An outstanding assemblage of rustic buildings from throughout Chelan County presents a vivid picture of what nineteenth-century life was like in central Washington. The "jail" was originally a cabin inhabited by an escaped convict from the federal penitentiary in Leavenworth, Kansas—who settled down in Leavenworth, Washington. Strange are the workings of the criminal mind. Inside the museum is a good collection of Indian artifacts from central Washington and elsewhere. The museum is open April through October, Monday through Saturday 10:00 a.m. to 4:30 p.m., Sunday 1:00 to 4:30 p.m. The pioneer village can be seen any time during daylight hours. Admission is $3 for adults, $1 for children under 12, maximum $5 per family.

While in pretty little Cashmere, with its refurbished turn-of-the-century storefronts, you might want to take the 15-minute free tour through the small family-run factory where they make Aplets and Cotlets. These all-natural fruit candies, sold throughout Washington and in gourmet shops elsewhere in the west, were invented by an Armenian immigrant who went into the candy business here after his Seattle restaurant failed in the 1920s. Besides the small-town success story, you'll get free samples and an irresistible opportunity to buy more. The Liberty Orchards Company Aplets Factory is at 117 Mission Street in Cashmere. Tour hours are May through December, Monday through Friday 8:00 a.m. to 5:00 p.m., Saturday and Sunday 10:00 a.m. to 4:00 p.m.; January through April, Monday through Friday, 8:00 a.m. to 12:00 noon and 1:00 to 5:00 p.m. Follow US 2/97 west for 10 more miles through the fruit orchards. When US 97 turns off to the south, unless you're in a hurry, keep going straight on US 2 for 4 miles to Leavenworth. Upon leaving Leavenworth, backtrack 4 miles to where US 97 turns south, and take that turn. Highway 97 climbs over the Wenatchee Mountains and descends to Ellensburg on the other side, a 51-mile trip. At Ellensburg, get on Interstate 90 eastbound and drive to the second exit, Interstate 82 southbound. It's 31 miles on I-82 to Yakima. If you wish to visit the Yakima Indian Cultural Center in Toppenish, take four-lane US 97, which parallels I-82, south for 15 miles and, after visiting the center, return by the same route to Yakima.

From Yakima, follow US 12 west for 18 miles to where Highway 410 forks off to the north. From there, it is 51 miles on Highway 410 through Mount Baker-Snoqualmie National Forest to the eastern boundary of Mount Rainier National Park at Cayuse Pass. You will not come to an entrance gate immediately upon entering the park. Follow Highway 123 south from Cayuse Pass for 12 miles to the Stevens Canyon entrance station, pay the $5-per-vehicle entrance fee, and turn west on Stevens Canyon Road, the most scenic in the park. About 12 more miles will bring you to the turnoff on your right to Paradise.

Sightseeing Highlights

▲▲**Leavenworth**—This self-styled "Bavarian village" used to be just another dry-side small town, half-deserted since the lumber mill closed down. Then, in 1965, residents noticed the similarity of the Bavarian Alps to their own alpine scenery and decided to refurbish their town in German style in a desperate attempt to attract tourists. I have to admit that when I first heard about this pseudo-Oberammergau on the American frontier, I thought it sounded like just another tacky tourist trap—but upon visiting, I discovered that I was wrong. It all works! From the main street's Disneyesque charm, to the view of the surrounding mountains from the idyllic riverside park, to the excellent pastry shops and restaurants with European-trained chefs, even to the gift shops bursting with Hummel figurines, souvenir beer steins, and fine wood carvings by German immigrant craftsmen, a single-minded identity and remarkable attention to detail have made Leavenworth a wonderful little one-of-a-kind Fantasyland. Okay, sometimes the Old World look clashes with mainstream America—just down the street from the world's only Tyrolean-style supermarket is a Thai restaurant behind a Bavarian facade. But it's all part of the fun. Leavenworth is jam-packed with oompah bands, beer, and tourist crowds for the Mai Fest in mid-May and the Autumn Leaf Festival (Oktoberfest) from the last weekend in September through the first weekend in October.

▲▲**Yakima Indian Nation Cultural Heritage Center**—This detour from the main route is unquestionably worthwhile for travelers who are interested in the native cultures of the Northwest. One's first impression of the Yakima tribe from the most populated part of the reservation, the 15-mile strip of US 97 between Yakima and

Toppenish, is of total assimilation: the Yakima people's homes, cars, commercial districts, and apple orchards look pretty much like everybody else's in this part of the state. But the Yakimas' cultural center is one of the finest Indian centers anywhere. The main visitors' attraction is the Yakima Nation Museum, where exhibits include wildlife dioramas; a full-size winter house made entirely of tule grass mats, where several Indian families might have lived during the cold months; a copy of the tribe's handwritten treaty with the United States; and talking rocks. Notice the diorama that depicts tribal ancestors fishing the salmon run at Celilo Falls on the Columbia River. Photographs of Indians fishing at the falls in more modern times are common in gift shops and visitor centers all along the Columbia. The falls themselves vanished forever in 1957 with the completion of the Dalles Dam. Besides the museum, the center has an extensive library on Native American subjects, a theater, and local handcrafts for sale. The center is open daily from 8:00 a.m. to 6:00 p.m. June through September, 8:00 a.m. to 5:00 p.m. the rest of the year. Admission to the museum is $2 per adult, $1 for children ages 5 to 18 and persons over the age of 54, with a maximum family rate of $5.

▲▲▲**Mount Rainier National Park**—Rising 14,410 feet above sea level, Mount Rainier is the tallest of the great Cascade Range volcanoes. Indians called this mountain Tahoma, meaning "the mountain that is God."

Mount Rainier is not dead but sleeping. It feels peaceful and timeless but smolders with hidden power. Steam hisses from fumaroles high on the glacier-clad cone, where stranded climbers have survived by huddling around the steam vents for warmth. Geologists predict that the volcano will erupt again—but probably not today. The bigger worry is mudflows, which can happen when the snowcap suddenly melts from the volcanic heat or heavy rain. On your way out of the park this afternoon, you'll see the aftermath of the 1947 Kautz Creek mudflow, which was up to 50 feet deep. About 5,800 years ago (only an eye blink in geologic time), such a mudflow buried the site of present-day Enumclaw 70 feet deep and reached almost as far the suburbs of Tacoma.

Hiking to the summit of Mount Rainier takes three days. Climbers need ice-climbing gear and an experienced guide on the steep glacier slopes. (Guided summit climbs and instruction can be arranged through Rainier Mountaineering Inc., 201 St. Helens, Tacoma, WA 98402, 627-6242.)

There are day hikes up the mountainside from Paradise for everyone from the intrepid to those who consider mountaineering a spectator sport. Easiest are the 1¼-mile Nisqually Vista Trail, commanding a view of the full length of Nisqually Glacier, and the 1½-mile Alta Vista Trail, through meadows of wildflowers to views of the Paradise River and distant snowcapped volcanoes to the south (Mount St. Helens and Mount Adams). Each of these walks begins at the visitors center and takes about an hour. The most ambitious and rewarding day hike from Paradise is the 6-mile, 5-hour Ice Caves Trail. It leads from the visitors center to the foot of Paradise Glaciers, where the summer melt flows in rivers under the ice, hollowing out caves big enough to walk into. For information on these and other hikes at Paradise, talk to the ranger at the hikers' desk in the visitors center. Paradise receives a 30-foot snow accumulation in the winter, and snow stays on the ground until June. It's an equally popular playground all year. In the snowy months, cross-country skis and snowshoes are available for rental at the Ski Shop near the National Park Inn at Longmire, between Paradise and the west entrance gate.

Food
If you want to stick around Leavenworth for lunch, there is an impressive array of possibilities. Not surprisingly, most feature German food. My nomination for the best in town is **Reiner's Gasthaus** at 829 Front Street, 548-5111. Prices are moderate. If sausage, sauerkraut, and spaetzel don't appeal, you'll find just plain American food—lots of it, at very reasonable prices—at the **Big Y Café** on the

main highway between Cashmere and Leavenworth. If you're traveling during the harvest season, after leaving Leavenworth and turning onto US 97, keep your eyes peeled for **Mom's First and Frank's Last Stand**, which has the edge over the area's many other fruit stands because of the home-baked fruit pies Mom sells there.

Yakima has several restaurants worth noting. **Gasperetti's** at 1013 North First Street, 248-0628, is probably the best Italian restaurant on the dry side of the Cascades. Similarly, **Santiago's** at 111 East Yakima Avenue, 453-1644, may be the best Mexican restaurant. I heartily recommend the restaurant at the **Yakima Indian Nation Cultural Heritage Center** in Toppenish, where entrées include the best buffalo burgers in the Northwest.

In Mount Rainier National Park, the **Longmire Country Store** beside the National Park Inn has a limited selection of picnic items, but campers would be wise to stock up on groceries in Leavenworth or Yakima.

The dining room at **Paradise Inn** serves breakfast from 7:00 to 9:00 a.m., lunch from 12:00 noon to 2:00 p.m., and dinner from 5:30 to 8:00 p.m. Sunday brunch hours are 11:00 a.m. to 2:30 p.m., during the months when the inn is open. (See Lodging.) Food service is also available at the **National Park Inn** at Longmire, as well as at the huge cafeteria in the **Paradise Visitors Center** (May through September and weekends in April and October), which can be crowded enough to keep you waiting an hour in line for a Coke.

Camping

The top campground choice in Mount Rainier National Park is **Cougar Rock Campground**, 2½ miles north of Longmire. At an elevation of 3,180 feet, this 200-site campground is open from late May through mid-October. You can camp year-round at the 18-site **Sunshine Point Campground** a short distance past the Nisqually entrance gate. Both campgrounds operate on a first-come, first-served basis, and neither has hookups, though Cougar Rock has a central dumping station. Camping fees are $6 per night at Cougar Rock, $5 at Sunshine Point.

Lodging

Paradise Inn, a historic 1917 lodge with massive stone fireplaces in the lobby, rents rooms at surprisingly reasonable rates: single or double for $90 with a private bath, $60 with a shared bath. The catch is that you need to make reservations far in advance. Prepayment for one night's lodgings is required to guarantee your reservation; then they'll send you a confirmation. (Hint: cancellations often make rooms available at the last minute. If you don't have a reservation, ask at the desk when you arrive at Paradise, and again around 4:00 p.m.) Paradise Inn only operates from the last week of May through the last week of September. Partway up the road to Paradise, at Longmire, is the smaller, cozier, recently renovated, and still rustic **National Park Inn**. Rates are a few dollars lower than at Paradise Inn. The reservation address is the same as for Paradise Inn. For information and reservations at either inn, call or write Mount Rainier Guest Services, P.O. Box 108, Ashford, WA 98304, (206) 569-2275.

MOUNT ST. HELENS NATIONAL MONUMENT

Today's route takes you from one volcano to the next, where—in startling contrast to the glaciers and alpine meadows of Mount Rainier—you will find proof on Mount St. Helens' barren, blasted slopes of the awesome power that lies sleeping beneath your feet wherever you go in the Cascade Mountains. You may wish to allow extra time for a short detour to visit Northwest Trek, the region's premier animal park.

Suggested Schedule

8:00 a.m.	Breakfast at Paradise Inn.
10:00 a.m.	Leave Mount Rainier National Park. Drive to Mount St. Helens.
12:00 noon	Picnic on Mount St. Helens at Meta Lake or Windy Ridge.
1:00 p.m	Hike Windy Ridge.
3:30 p.m.	Drive to Cougar.
5:00 p.m.	Check into your accommodations in Cougar or drive to Portland and spend tonight there.

Travel Route: Mount Rainier to Mount St. Helens (145 miles) to Portland (57 miles)

From Paradise, return to the main park road and proceed east for about 15 scenic miles to the intersection with WA 123. Turn right (south), and in 6 more miles, just after leaving the national park, the road merges with US 12. Continue south on US 12 to the small town of Randle, a distance of 26 miles. Turn left (south) at Randle onto paved Forest Road 25. Follow FR 25 south for 20 miles to the junction with paved FR 99, which climbs for 17 steep miles to dead-end at Windy Ridge.

Upon leaving Windy Ridge, go back downhill to FR 25 and turn right (south), driving 20 miles to the Pine Creek Information Station. Turn right (west) on WA 503 and proceed 18 more miles to Cougar. Forest roads to other areas of Mount St. Helens National Monument, including Lava Canyon and Ape Cave, leave FR 90 between the Pine Creek Information Station and Cougar.

When you're ready to go on to Portland—whether this afternoon or tomorrow morning—continue west on WA 503 along the shores of Lake Yale and Merwyn Reservoir. Driving 29 miles will bring you to Interstate 5 at the town of Woodland, just 28 miles north of Portland. Take the Burnside exit and cross the Burnside Bridge into downtown Portland. The waterfront park and the starting point for the walking tour outlined in Day 12 are just south on Front Street as soon as you cross the bridge.

Sightseeing Highlight

▲▲▲Mount St. Helens National Monument—While Mount Rainier is the tallest of the great volcanoes in the Cascade Range, Mount St. Helens attained equal fame on May 18, 1980, by becoming the shortest (8,365 feet). On that date, practically without warning, the mountain blew off 1,300 feet of its summit, sending up a 15-mile-high plume of rock, ash, and smoke that darkened the sky over much of eastern Washington and portions of Idaho and Montana, devastating 235 square miles of landscape on the east slope of the mountain and claiming 57 human lives along with 221 homes and 17 miles of railroad track. It presented television audiences across the nation with an awesome new image of nature's potential for sudden violence.

Before the blast, environmentalists had been fighting to save the forest around Mount St. Helens, legendary home of the Sasquatch or "Bigfoot," from timber operations. In 1982, 110,330 acres of the Gifford Pinchot National Forest encompassing the volcano were set aside as Mount St. Helens National Monument. The trees, of course, had been destroyed more thoroughly than if they had been clear-cut—burned, blown flat, and buried in tons of volcanic ash.

Today, new life is beginning to spring from the ash-enriched slopes. The most common vegetation is fireweed, which sets the slopes ablaze in brilliant magenta

Mount Rainier and Mount St. Helens

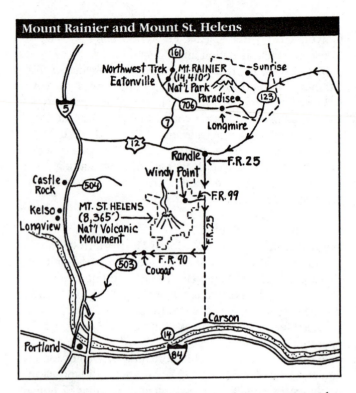

during the summer months. The once-bare mountainside is also painted seasonally with blue lupine, purple penstemon, and a host of other colorful flowers. Frogs and fish now live in most of the lakes and attract wading birds such as the great blue heron. Here and there, tiny new evergreen seedlings are beginning to sprout from the ashes. National monument status ensures that as the forests slowly return to the mountaintop over the next few generations, they and their animal inhabitants will be safe from lumberjacks' chainsaws forever.

Formerly an out-of-the-way place with a handful of mountain cabins and small resort ranches, Mount St. Helens now attracts more than 2 million visitors a year. The main road route around the east side of the mountain, which provides the best access to the blast area at Windy Ridge, has recently been paved.

On Windy Ridge, the paved road dead-ends at the top

ridgeline, where a long, steep stairway climbs to a hilltop that affords the best view of Spirit Lake, a thousand feet below. The lake was there before the eruption, a remote fishing area with a few summer cabins on its shores. After the blast, its surface rose 200 feet as huge amounts of volcanic ash filled it. Today, much of the surface is covered with logjams of trees blown down by the eruptions. The shore of the lake can be reached by foot on Harmony Trail, a strenuous 1-mile hike that descends 600 feet to the lakeshore from the trailhead at Harmony Viewpoint on Windy Ridge Road. From another trailhead nearby, an easy ½-mile paved trail leads to Meta Lake, a little "island" of forest that was sheltered from the volcano's blast by a cliff and now provides an oasis of green in the midst of desolation.

The ultimate view of the Mount St. Helens blast area is from the unpaved, hikers- and mountain bikers-only trail that continues beyond the parking area at the top of Windy Ridge. The trail continues for three miles across the face of the crater, providing a constant view of the St. Helens summit from just 4½ miles away. At the end, it joins the Boundary Trail, which goes all the way around the volcano. It's a dry, sun-blasted hike—be sure to take water.

Forest Road 83, which leaves FR 90 midway between the Pine Creek Information Station and Cougar on the south side of the mountain, affords access to a network of unpaved roads and foot trails on the south side of the mountain. Ape Cave Geological Site, reached from a turn-off two miles up this road, is the longest lava tube in North America—12,810 feet long. It was formed during volcanic activity about 2,000 years ago. Contrary to what you might think, the cave was not named for the Sasquatch that some people claim to have seen in this area but for the St. Helens Apes, a local hiking club that discovered the cave in the 1940s. (*They* were named for the legendary Sasquatch.) If you want to explore the depths of the cave, wear warm clothes and bring a flashlight. Lights can be rented at the cave entrance during the summer season. Other attractions in the same area include several trails into the Loowit Trail around Mount St. Helens at approximately timberline (4,800 feet), as well as Lava Canyon Recreation Area, where a trail leads one-half mile to a waterfall that plunges over an ancient lava flow, then continues another 2½ strenuous miles up a mudflow-scoured canyon, where it sometimes narrows and edges along steep cliffs.

The roads around the south and east sides of Mount St. Helens are snowbound from October to late May or early June. You can get current road and hiking information from the Woods Creek Information Station south of Randle.

Sightseeing flights over Mount St. Helens are available at general aviation airports at Silver Lake and Kelso-Longview. Expensive but worth every penny, the flights range from 30 to 90 minutes and cost from $40 to $100 per person.

Camping

The public campground most convenient to Mount St. Helens is **Seaquest State Park**, across the road from the Mount St. Helens vistors' center, 5 miles east of the Castle Rock exit from I-5. Sites cost $7 a night, $2.50 more with full hookups. The park has nature trails and a beach on Silver Lake. There is no access to Mount St. Helens itself from this road. There are also small national forest campgrounds at Cougar and nearby Merrill Lake.

Food and Lodging

Since most visitors come to Mount St. Helens on day trips from Seattle and Portland, the lodging situation around the national monument has not kept pace with the area's burgeoning tourism. Roadside motels, fast-food places, and family restaurants can be found near most exits from Interstate 5. However, if you have not made reservations near Mount St. Helens, it's as easy to drive on into Portland this evening as to search for a motel along the interstate.

In the small country community of Cougar, the **Lone Fir Resort** offers motel units and cabins—not luxurious but in a beautiful mountain setting, with rooms starting at $38 a night. The resort is small, so reservations are essential. Call (206) 238-5210. In a slightly higher price range, **Monfort's Bed & Breakfast** offers new, comfortable rooms and a full country breakfast. Call (206) 238-5229.

Itinerary Option: Northwest Trek

Animal lovers and anyone traveling with children will want to allow several extra hours in their itinerary to visit Northwest Trek, east of Mount Rainier. This outstanding wildlife park, a division of Tacoma's Metropolitan Park District, offers a close-up look at native northwestern wildlife roaming free in 435 acres of meadows and forest. A 45-minute tram tour runs hourly through the park. Sit on the left-hand side for the best view of mountain goats, bighorn sheep, bison, Roosevelt elk, caribou, and, if you're lucky, a moose. See predators such as bears, wolves, mountain lions, and eagles in their separate enclosures while you're waiting for the tour.

Northwest Trek's most numerous residents, Pennsylvania wild turkeys, are not native to this region. They were brought here by state government as a pilot project to see whether they could be introduced in the wilds of Washington as a game bird. They flourished and practically overran the park. With the decision to set their turkeys free in other areas, the park staff drew media snickers because they couldn't catch the birds. The final solution was alcohol-spiked grain, on the theory that turkeys are easier to catch when they're drunk. It worked, and you stand a good chance of seeing the immigrant fowl elsewhere in western Washington during this tour.

To get to Northwest Trek, drive west on WA 706 for 31 miles from Paradise. At Elbe, turn north on WA 7 and go 10 miles to where WA 161 turns off to the right. Follow WA 161 for 6 miles, through the town of Eatonville to Northwest Trek. Upon leaving the park, return to WA 7 and drive south for 27 miles to Morton. Take US 12 east for 17 miles to Randle, where you rejoin the main travel route to Mount St. Helens.

Northwest Trek opens at 9:30 a.m. daily from mid-

February through October 31, Friday through Sunday only the rest of the year. Closing times vary. Admission is $7.50 for adults, $6.50 for senior citizens, $5 for students ages 5 to 17, and $3 for children ages 3 and 4.

PORTLAND

After taking the scenic route from the Canadian border to the Washington-Oregon state line in the past few days, through some of the most fabulous wilderness in America, you deserve a break today. You have as much to look forward to on this trip as you have to look back on. Before heading off on the second half of this Northwest trip, into the even more remote backcountry of Oregon, take a day-long "vacation from your vacation" to rest up, replenish your trip provisions, and explore the state's largest city.

Suggested Schedule	
Morning	Drive from Cougar to Portland if you didn't do so yesterday afternoon.
Afternoon	Take it easy. Enjoy a walking tour of downtown Portland. Visit the rose gardens. Catch up on your shopping.
Evening	Take it easy some more.

Portland: A Walking Tour

On first impression, Portland may seem like Seattle's kid sister. A little smaller (pop. 366,000), bordered by narrower bodies of water (the Columbia and Willamette rivers), in the shadow of a somewhat smaller volcano (Mt. Hood, 11,239 feet above sea level), Portland surpasses Seattle in at least two respects: first, it's older (founded in 1844, it was the departure point when Seattle's founding fathers started their journey north seven years later); and second, it receives more rainfall (37.6 inches a year).

An easy-to-find starting point for a brief exploration of downtown Portland is **Governor Tom McCall Waterfront Park**, named for Oregon's environmentalist, antigrowth governor of the early 1970s, who launched a publicity campaign inviting tourists to visit Washington, Idaho, Montana—any place but Oregon. The park runs along the banks of the Willamette River for 25 blocks, the entire eastern edge of downtown. Near the south end of

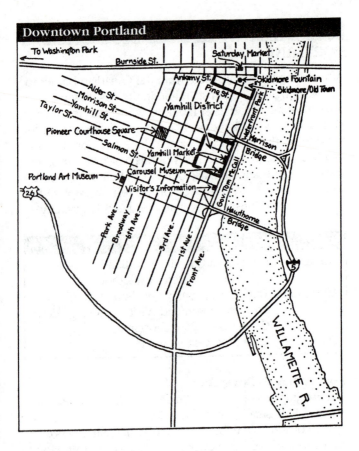

the park is the Visitors Information Center pavilion. Stop there for walking tour brochures of the Yamhill and Skidmore/Old Town historic districts, as well as information on performing arts and other entertainment.

Stroll Portland's original commercial area, the **Yamhill District**, a six-square-block area beginning two blocks north of the visitor center, along Taylor, Yamhill, and Morrison streets between Front and Third avenues. The Yamhill District's buildings with their unusual wrought-iron facades had deteriorated sadly before restoration began in the late 1970s and chic retail establishments moved in. The centerpiece of the district is **Yamhill Marketplace**, a 1982 building designed to be compatible

with the surrounding historic architecture, where a produce market coexists with upscale restaurants, shops, and
art galleries.

A seven-block walk north through the waterfront park
brings you to the **Skidmore/Old Town District**, where
historic buildings similar in style to those in the Yamhill
District are scattered between Pine and Davis streets
within three blocks of the river. The Skidmore Fountain,
on Ankeny Street one block from the waterfront past
Ankeny Park and Arcade, is a well-known Portland landmark. This 1888 bronze and granite masterpiece was the
first of Portland's famous fountains, which now seem to
be everywhere. Across the railroad tracks from the fountain is the thoroughly gentrified New Market Block.
Formerly the New Market Theater, it was a 1,200-seat
center for the city's performing arts—on the second floor
of a farmers' market! Also of interest in Skidmore/Old
Town is the old Erickson's Saloon, where sailors and
sophisticates used to rub elbows along a 684-foot bar
before Prohibition shut it down. Today the building
houses the **American Advertising Museum**, where ads
from early newspaper days to the TV era are immortal-
ized. The museum is open Wednesday through Friday
11:00 a.m .to 5:00 p.m., Saturday and Sunday noon to
5:00 p.m. Admission is $3, children ages 6 to 12 $1.50.

If you're visiting Portland on the weekend, don't miss
the Saturday Market under the Burnside Bridge, a block
north of Ankeny Park and the Skidmore Fountain. It's the
city's liveliest assemblage of artists, craftsmen, and street
musicians. Hours are 10:00 a.m. to 5:00 p.m. Saturday and
11:00 a.m. to 4:30 p.m. Sunday.

To return to the point where you started your downtown tour, proceed west on Ankeny to Southwest Fifth
Avenue and turn left (south). As you pass the Georgia
Pacific Building in the 900 block of Fifth, you can't help
but notice the white marble sculpture entitled *The Quest*,
which residents have nicknamed "Three Groins in the
Fountain." Controversial public art and architecture have
come to characterize Portland in recent years, and several
of the best (or worst) examples can be found around

Pioneer Courthouse Square, to your right, bordered by Sixth Avenue, Broadway, Morrison, and Yamhill. Amid the wrought-iron gates and fences, neoclassical columns (including an intentionally collapsed column with a chessboard on top), and purple-tiled waterfall, 48,000 bricks bear the names of donors who helped make it all possible. The adjoining transit mall between Fifth and Sixth avenues is a people watcher's paradise. The ultimate offbeat building downtown (or, for that matter, anywhere) is the Portland Building at 1120 SW Fifth Avenue. Designed by Michael Graves, billed as "the first major postmodern structure erected in the United States," it's pink, yellow, blue, and bizarre. On the Fifth Avenue side of the Portland Building is the kneeling statue of Portlandia, the largest hammered copper sculpture erected since the Statue of Liberty.

From Portlandia, you can walk back west five blocks to the waterfront park. Or, to extend your downtown walking tour, head west to Broadway, then south (left) to Salmon Street. At the corner, under the Jackson Tower Clock decorated with flags and lights, turn right and go one block to the north end of the Park Blocks (also called "the Boulevard"), and go three blocks south along the walkway to the Oregon Art Institute, where the **Portland Museum of Art** is located. Among the museum's exhibits are exceptional collections of Oriental and Pacific Northwest Indian art. It is open Tuesday through Saturday from 11:00 a.m. to 5:00 p.m. and Sunday from 1:00 to 5:00 p.m., as well as 5:00 to 9:00 p.m. on the first Thursday of each month. Admission is $4.50 for adults, $2.50 for students age 6 and up. No admission fee is charged on the first Thursday of the month after 4:00 p.m. (A good inexpensive souvenir typifying Portland's offbeat attitude toward art is the now-classic "Expose Yourself to Art" poster available at the museum and elsewhere. The guy in the trenchcoat flashing the statue is rumored to have been Portland's mayor at the time the photo was taken.) From the art museum, a nine-block walk east on Jefferson or Madison will bring you back to the south end of the waterfront park near the Hawthorne Bridge.

In this tour I've kept my suggestions for visiting Portland brief. If you're planning to spend extra time in the city, you'll learn about dozens of other sightseeing possibilities at the visitors information center in Governor Tom McCall Waterfront Park. Especially worth visiting is a cluster of attractions around Washington Park, west of downtown on Burnside Street or US 26. The **Washington Park Zoo** is open daily (weekends only in winter) from 9:30 a.m. with variable closing hours, adults $5.50, children under 12 and seniors over 65 $4. Next to the zoo is the **World Forestry Center**, where you'll learn everything you may ever want to know about the lumber industry (a looming presence in any Pacific Northwest tour) from exhibits that include a 70-foot talking tree; open daily 10:00 a.m. to 5:00 p.m., adults $3, children ages 6 to 18 and seniors over 65 $2. Portland is famed for its roses, and while they grow in most city parks as well as private yards throughout the city, one of the world's finest rose gardens is the **International Rose Test Garden** in Washington Park, where over 400 varieties have been cultivated continuously since 1917. It is open at all times during daylight hours, free.

Camping

The best public campground in the Portland area is **Ainsworth State Park** at the western end of the Columbia Gorge Scenic Highway (see tomorrow's Travel Route and Sightseeing Highlights). There are 63 campsites, all but 5 with full hookups. Camping fees are $10 during the summer season, $7 off-season. The park also has a trailhead for a portion of the Columbia Gorge Trail.

Lodging

The perfect location in downtown Portland is the **Riverside Inn** at Morrison and Front Avenue, facing Governor Tom McCall Waterfront Park on the edge of Old Town. Rates are in the $72 to $87 range. For reservations, call (503) 221-0711, toll-free (800) 648-6440.

You may feel that you deserve a serious splurge after the past two nights camping out in the boondocks—bearing in mind that tomorrow you'll be heading even deeper into empty dry-side country where lodgings are practically nonexistent. Contrast is the key to an exciting vacation, right? The longtime lap of luxury in downtown Portland is the **Heathman Hotel**, a National Historic Landmark at SW Broadway and Salmon Street, next door to the Center for the Performing Arts and a short stroll from the art museum. This hotel has everything—24-hour concierge service, a video library, a grand piano and fireplace in the lobby, guest rooms furnished in Ming, Regency, or Biedermeier style, and one of Portland's finest restaurants. Rates start at $160 double. For reservations, call (503) 241-4100 or (800) 551-0011 nationwide. For more contemporary upscale accommodations, the place to go is the **RiverPlace Hotel**, a modern luxury hotel with rooms overlooking the waterfront promenade, 1510 SW Harbor Way, (503) 228-3233. Room rates start at $165 a night.

More affordable elegance is to be found at **Portland's White House**, a B&B across the river at 1914 NE 22nd Avenue, (503) 287-7131. This restored turn-of-the-century mansion has Greek columns, a circular driveway with a fountain, and an uncanny resemblance to the president's house in Washington. Surprisingly reasonable rates, in the $70 to $90 range, include a gourmet breakfast. There are only six guest rooms, so make reservations well in advance.

Close to downtown and in a lower price range, the **Mallory Motor Hotel** at SW 15th and Yamhill offers rooms starting at $55 a night. Call (503) 226-2970, toll-free (800) 228-8657.

Portland International Hostel is located at 3031 SE Hawthorne Boulevard, with easy access to downtown on the #14 Tri-Met bus line. Dormitory beds cost under $10 for AYH members. Desk hours are 8:00 to 9:30 a.m. and 5:00 to 10:00 p.m. Reservations are a good idea. Call (503) 236-3380.

Food

Perhaps downtown Portland's most popular restaurant (at least the most often recommended) is **Jake's Famous Crawfish** at 401 South 12th. Jake's has been serving local crawfish since 1892 and also offers a large selection of other seafood specialties. Hours are Monday through Friday 11:00 a.m. to 3:00 p.m., Monday through Thursday 5:00 to 11:00 p.m., Friday and Saturday 5:00 p.m. to midnight, and Sunday 5:00 to 10:00 p.m. Prices are moderate. Call 226-1419.

For Japanese cuisine in Portland, try **Zen**, 910 SW Salmon, open Monday through Friday 11:30 a.m. to 2:00 p.m. and Monday through Saturday 5:00 to 10:00 p.m., 222-3065; or the popular sushi bar at **Bush Garden**, 900 SW Morrison, open Monday through Friday 11:30 a.m. to 2:00 p.m., Monday through Saturday 5:00 to 10:00 p.m., and Sunday 5:00 to 9:00 p.m., 226-7181.

Inexpensive and unusual are **Chang's Mongolian Grill**, 1 SW Third, open daily from 11:30 a.m. to 2:20 p.m. and 5:00 to 9:40 p.m., 243-1991; **Saigon Express** (Vietnamese), 309 West Burnside, open Monday through Saturday from 11:30 a.m. to 11:00 p.m., 227-7499; and **Alexis** (Greek), 215 West Burnside, open Monday through Friday 11:30 a.m. to 2:00 p.m., Monday through Thursday 5:00 to 10:00 p.m., Friday and Saturday 5:00 to 11:00 p.m., and Sunday 4:30 to 9:30 p.m., 224-8577. For a good, really low-priced breakfast or lunch downtown (breakfast served all day), stop at the **Bijou Café**, 132 SW Third Avenue, open 7:00 a.m. to 3:00 p.m., 222-3187.

Nightlife
Portland's top comedy club is **The Last Laugh Comedy Club** at 426 NW Sixth, 295-2844. This Las Vegas-style showroom serves up nationally known comedy acts along with dinner and cocktails nightly from 6:00 p.m. to 12:30 a.m. Prices are reasonable. Other intriguing nightclubs include the tropical-style **Key Largo** at 31 NW First Avenue, 223-9919, with an eclectic schedule of dance music, and the nearby **Starry Night**, 8 NW Sixth Avenue, similar in its range of popular music offerings. Downtown art galleries are open late on the first Thursday of each month, and many host wine-and-cheese artist receptions.

THE COLUMBIA GORGE

Today's route follows the Columbia River eastward for 100 miles. On the first part of the drive, you'll view the magnificent waterfalls along the Columbia Gorge Scenic Highway. Later, you'll see a unique mansion-museum, a piece of the 1920s Paris art scene improbably transplanted to the wild western frontier by the same man who built the scenic drive. End your day on the slopes of Mount Hood.

Suggested Schedule

8:30 a.m.	Leave Portland.
9:00 a.m.	Start your Columbia Gorge drive with an overview from Crown Point.
9:30 a.m.	Drive the scenic highway, stopping at each waterfall.
11:00 a.m.	Visit Bonneville Dam.
12:00 noon	Drive on to Maryhill.
1:30 p.m.	Visit Maryhill Museum of Art.
3:00 p.m.	Visit Sam Hill's Stonehenge.
3:30 p.m.	Return to Hood River.
4:30 p.m.	Drive to Government Camp.
5:30 p.m.	Find a campsite or check in at Timberline Lodge.

Travel Route: Portland to Maryhill (107 miles) to Mount Hood (87 miles)

From Portland, follow Interstate 84 (which meets I-5 just across the river from downtown) east for 16 miles to the second Troutdale exit. This is the beginning of the Columbia Gorge Scenic Highway. Twenty-two relaxing miles and several scenic stops later, you'll rejoin the interstate. Just 5 miles on, you'll come to Bonneville Dam (exit 40).

Four miles east of the dam, at Cascade Locks, cross the river into Washington on the Bridge of the Gods. The toll bridge (50 cents; towed vehicles 25 cents per axle) was so named because of an Indian legend that says a vast natural bridge, built by gods, once spanned the river (though not at this site). If true, it was by far the largest natural bridge on earth. As the story goes, the legendary bridge collapsed to create Celilo Falls, the falls depicted in the salmon-fishing diorama at the Yakima Nation Museum; you can see photographs and postcards of Indians fishing there at any gift shop along the Columbia. Don't look for the falls themselves, though. Like the original Bridge of the Gods, they have vanished forever into legend, flooded by the completion of the Dalles Dam in 1957.

Washington Highway 14, slower but quieter, follows the north bank of the Columbia River for 60 miles to Maryhill. It is known as the Lewis and Clark Trail.

After visiting Maryhill, cross the river back into Oregon and take Interstate 84 west for 40 fast miles to Hood River. Turn south there on Highway 35 and drive 47 miles, climbing along the west side of Mount Hood, to Government Camp and Timberline Lodge.

Sightseeing Highlights

▲▲▲**Columbia Gorge Scenic Highway**—In 1913, when Sam Hill started building his highway up the Columbia, he paved this stretch first. The spectacular roadside beauty generated enough excitement to convince politicians to finance the rest of the road. When the highway was widened to become Interstate 84, this stretch was by-passed and preserved as a scenic detour. The best scenery is along the first few miles from the eastern end of the highway, in Mount Hood National Forest. Farther down toward Troutdale, where most land is under private ownership, some local residents chafe under tight restrictions on development, imposed to prevent, as a recent letter to the editor in a Portland newspaper put it, "wall-to-wall bed and breakfasts."

First take the ¾-mile side road up to Vista House at Crown Point, a hilltop overlook that commands a 30-mile view up the river and gorge, where you can look down at the scenic highway you're about to travel. At Latourell Falls, a short hiking trail lets you walk close enough to the 224-foot cataract to feel the spray and even climb

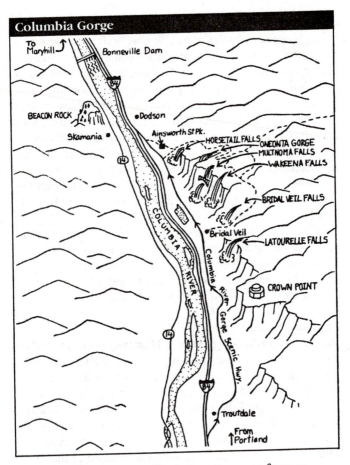

Columbia Gorge

behind it. Wahkeenee Falls derives its name from an
Indian word meaning "most beautiful." Multnomah Falls,
at 620 feet one of the highest waterfalls in the United
States, is the most developed stop on the route, with a
visitor center, a gift shop, and a paved walkway to a foot-
bridge midway up the falls. Next comes Oneonta Gorge,
a stop that many sightseers bypass because there's no
waterfall—but don't miss it. The fantastic assortment of
plant life to be seen along the short nature trail between
the sheer cliffs includes subspecies that exist no place else
on earth. Horsetail Falls is a good place to access the east
end of the Columbia Gorge hiking trail system.

Justly famous and next door to Portland, the waterfalls
along the Columbia Gorge Scenic Highway can be crowded
beyond belief in July and August, as well as on any weekend when the weather is fair. Here's a secret for escaping
the mob: hike. A trail parallels the highway, a few hundred feet uphill where it's peaceful and quiet. For a fine
two- to three-hour hike, park at Horsetail Falls and clam-
ber up the short, steep trail to the top of the falls, where
you'll join the main gorge trail. Cross the creek and hike
west, skirting the rim of Oneonta Gorge, and continue
until you reach Multnomah Falls. Descend there and walk
back up the road to where you parked. The trail is a little
more than 3 miles long, and the road distance back from
Multnomah Falls to Horsetail Falls is 2½ miles. If you want
a longer hike, deeper into the dense wilderness above the
gorge, first stop at the Multnomah Falls gift shop to buy
the $1.25 *Forest Trails of the Columbia Gorge* map pub-
lished by the U.S. Forest Service. It describes 36 trails in
the area—a total of 166 miles of hiking, along most of
which you'll never meet another human being.

▲▲**Bonneville Dam**—The dam, built between 1933 and
1937 at a cost of nearly $89 million, impounds a 48-mile-
long reservoir on the Columbia and produces 1,084,900
kilowatts of electricity. You can ride an elevator down to
see the hydropower generators. The five-level Bradford
Island Visitor Center in the middle of the dam is the
largest visitor center on the river. Even if the dam itself
holds no interest for you, other exhibits here will. They
range from ancient Indian rock effigies and Lewis and
Clark memorabilia to underwater fish-viewing windows.
This visitor center, as well as a second, smaller one on
the Washington shore, is open daily from 8:00 a.m. to
6:00 p.m. Memorial Day to July 3, 8:00 a.m. to 8:00 p.m.
July 4 to Labor Day, and 9:00 a.m. to 5:00 p.m. the rest
of the year. Admission is free.

Also of interest during your Bonneville Dam visit are the
methods they've devised to let both people and fish travel
the river despite the massive wall of concrete. Watch the
operation of the navigation locks that allow barges and
other craft, as well as log floats, through the dam. When

salmon are running, the sight of myriad fish climbing over the dam on the four fish ladders (pools arranged like staircases to let the fish leap from one to the next) attracts hordes of spectators. Steelhead run from July through October; chinook have three separate runs between mid-April and October. Between 700,000 and 1,000,000 adult fish climb the ladders each year as they travel upriver to spawn and die. From 30 million to 50 million young fish travel down the fish ladders each year on their journey to the ocean.

Besides being tourist attractions, the fish ladders and fish counters are vital parts of a 1980 federal plan to halt and reverse the massive depletion of salmon caused by this and other dams in previous decades. The same plan is likely to halt at least 200 proposed hydroelectric projects in the Northwest.

Lewis and Clark Trail—Washington State Highway 14, along the north bank of the Columbia River, is known as the Lewis and Clark Trail. While the explorers traveled down the Columbia in dugout canoes, paddling back upstream proved such hard work that they traded their canoes to Indians at The Dalles for horses and rode up the route you'll drive today.

U.S. Army Captains Meriwether Lewis and William Clark were commissioned by Thomas Jefferson to explore the newly purchased Louisiana Territory. Starting near St. Louis on May 14, 1804, they traveled across what would become Missouri, Iowa, Nebraska, South and North Dakota, Montana, Idaho, and eastern Washington before reaching the Columbia River in October 1805. They found the Pacific Ocean a month later and started back the following spring. Their 8,000-mile round-trip took 861 days.

Today, history buffs can find historical markers commemorating Lewis and Clark's progress at Horsethief Lake State Park, The Dalles, Beacon Rock State Park, and Lewis and Clark State Park, as well as exhibits on the expedition at the Bonneville Dam visitor center. More Lewis and Clark memorabilia are at the High Desert Museum near Bend (Day 15) and at Ecola State Park, Seaside, Fort Clatsop, and Fort Canby (Day 19).

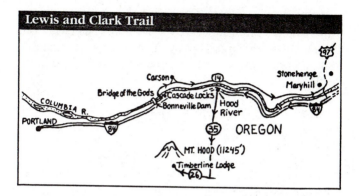

Lewis and Clark Trail

▲▲▲**Maryhill Museum of Art**—This classically French, concrete château in the middle of nowhere, where peacocks stroll on acres of landscaped lawn amid barren hills overlooking the Columbia River, was the creation of turn-of-the-century visionary capitalist Sam Hill (as in, "What the Sam Hill is he up to now?"). Hill was an assistant to railroad baron James J. Hill—no relation until Sam married James's daughter, Mary Hill, for whom the estate was named. Sam bought 7,000 acres here with plans to start a town. In 1914, he began building this mansion to preside over the new community, but when his real estate scheme collapsed, Sam lost interest in his unfinished home.

Sam traveled to Europe fifty times selling railroad bonds to royalty. During these trips he befriended Loie Fuller, the Chicago-born Folies Bergere star and pioneer of modern dance. Loie convinced Sam that he should turn his white-elephant mansion into an art museum. She sold Sam a large number of works by her friend Auguste Rodin (often called the greatest sculptor since Michelangelo), while Sam prevailed on his friend, Queen Marie of Romania, to travel to the high desert of southern Washington to dedicate the museum.

Maryhill Museum displays the results of this unlikely quartet's efforts in three floors of well-focused and fascinating exhibits that would do credit to any art museum, anywhere. Rodin bronzes and plasters (including a study for his familiar *The Thinker*) fill most of the upper floor, while the ground-floor main hall contains the Romanian royal furniture and memorabilia. Other galleries feature Sam's excellent Indian basketry collection, chess sets from around the world, and an array of small, powerful paintings and prints that depict the destruction of Europe in World War I.

The art museum is open daily from March 15 through November 15, 9:00 a.m. to 5:00 p.m., adults $4, senior citizens $3.50, students ages 6 to 16 $1.50, children age 5 and under free.

Sam Hill also envisioned and built the first highway up the Columbia Gorge. Today, the part of his road that has not been preserved as the Columbia Gorge Scenic Highway has become Interstate 84, which you see across the river in Oregon. Sam wanted to build his road on the Washington side but couldn't convince state congressmen that the idea had merit. That's why you're here and the freeway is over there.

▲**Stonehenge**—As a pioneer road builder, Sam Hill loved concrete. And the horrifying World War I paintings on the lower level of his art museum attest that he also hated war. The two passions united in this huge, strange artifact—a full-sized exact replica of Stonehenge, constructed entirely of cast concrete, sits on a hilltop overlooking the Columbia River as a memorial to the World War I dead of Klickitat County. Hill's tomb is here. The road up to Stonehenge starts right next to the campground entrance at Maryhill State Park.

Camping

There are two public campgrounds at the small resort community of Government Camp. **Trillium Lake Campground**, 2¼ miles southeast of the highway intersection on US 26 and then 1¼ miles south on Forest Road 2656, offers swimming and sites for larger RVs and charges $6 to $8 per night. **Still Creek Campground**, 1G miles southeast on US 26 and one-half mile south on Forest Road 2650, is limited to tents and RVs 16 feet in length or less. The camping fee is $8 a night. Both are open from Memorial Day to Labor Day only.

Food and Lodging

While there are plenty of freeway eateries in Cascade Locks, Hood River, and The Dalles, there's not much in the way of food along the Lewis and Clark Trail until you reach the Maryhill Art Museum, which has a gourmet snack bar on the lower level.

Timberline Lodge, a 1937 National Historic Landmark lodge at 6,000 feet elevation on the slope of Mount Hood, 6 miles up a well-marked road near Government Camp, is noteworthy for the northwestern artwork on display as well as the craftsmanship of the decor and furnishings, products of a depression-era WPA program to support artists. Today it serves primarily as a ski lodge but is open—and popular—year-round. Rates range from $86 to $101 a night, and reservations are essential. Call (503) 231-7979, or toll-free 231-5400 in Portland, (800) 452-1335 within Oregon, or (800) 547-1406 nationwide. A cafeteria nearby offers a quicker and less costly alternative to dining at the lodge.

JOHN DAY COUNTRY

Prehistoric rhinoceroses and guru Bhagwan Sri Rajneesh both used to live in central Oregon, but they don't any more. Hardly anybody else does, either, as you'll discover while traveling the stark labyrinth of John Day Country. Experience surrealistic prehistory today, climaxing in a close encounter with a saber-toothed cat in a bright blue landscape.

Suggested Schedule

7:30 a.m.	Getting an early start from Government Camp, drive west on US 26.
9:00 a.m.	Visit Shaniko, then drive on through Antelope (don't blink or you'll miss it).
9:30 a.m.	Take a short hike at the Clarno Unit of John Day Fossil Beds.
10:00 a.m.	Drive on to Blue Basin, John Day Fossil Beds.
12:00 noon	Walk the Island in Time Trail.
1:00 p.m.	Drive to Sheep Rock Visitor Center.
1:30 p.m.	See the visitor center.
2:00 p.m.	Drive to Painted Hills Unit.
2:45 p.m.	Hike the Painted Hills.
3:30 p.m.	Drive to Bend.
7:00 p.m.	Arrive in Bend.

Travel Route: Government Camp to John Day Fossil Beds to Bend (290 miles)

This is the longest and loneliest single-day drive on the 22-day itinerary. You could easily skip it and follow US Highways 26 and 97 directly from Government Camp to Bend, a 163-mile, three-hour drive. But by doing so, you would miss experiencing the rugged beauty of the Oregon desert.

Instead, drive 13 miles southeast of Government Camp on US 26 and watch for Highway 216, which forks off to the left. Follow Highway 216 for 29 miles to Maupin. From

Maupin, take the two-lane highway that leaves town to the north and then, in less than a mile, forks east toward Shaniko, 26 miles away, where you'll briefly intersect US 97.

From Shaniko, follow US 218, which leaves town to the south, 8 miles to Antelope and 11 more miles to the Clarno Unit of John Day Fossil Beds. Both stretches of road—from Shaniko to Antelope and Antelope to Clarno—appear straight on the map, but don't be fooled into thinking it's a short drive. This is rugged country with wild altitude changes. Especially in a motor home, the road will seem much longer than its actual mileage. It's your introduction to the roads of John Day Country—empty, fun to drive, but not for those in a hurry.

From the remote Clarno Unit, it's another 20 miles to Fossil, the biggest town in these parts (which is to say, there are buildings on both sides of the street). Be sure to fill the gas tank in Fossil. You won't see another service station for 140 miles.

From Fossil, follow Highway 19 south for about 60 miles to Blue Basin. If you camped at Shelton Wayside last night, it's all downhill to the John Day River; the last 40 miles, along the riverbank, are easier and faster than the roads you've been on. Watch for the Blue Basin parking area on your left.

Seems like they haven't had many people in these parts to name things after. Practically everything in this part of the state—referred to as John Day Country—is called John Day (except for the town of Mount Vernon, which was named after a horse). John Day Fossil Beds and the towns of John Day and Dayville were so named because they were on the John Day River. John Day himself was a hunter on a John Jacob Astor expedition that came west in 1811. He was separated from his party, and Indians robbed him of his "possibles." He was rescued, but later, when he returned to the site where he'd been found, Day's mind snapped and he went mad. So his companions named the river after him.

From Blue Basin, it's a short drive to the John Day Fossil Beds Visitor Center at Cant Ranch.

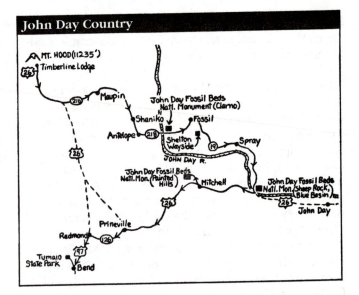

John Day Country

A short distance south from the ranch is the junction with US 26. Turn right (west), and 28 miles will bring you to the turnoff on the right to the Painted Hills Unit of John Day Fossil Beds. It's 6 miles in to the painted hills themselves.

Returning to US 26, continue west for another 71 miles to Redmond, passing through some thoroughly logged parts of Ochoco National Forest. Chief Ochoco and his band of about 50 followers, who had never signed a treaty with the United States, lived in the forest during the 1880s until the chief was shot and killed by members of a notorious Prineville vigilante group known as the Izee Sheepshooters Association. So the government named the forest after him.

At Redmond, turn south on busy US 97, and 16 more miles will bring you to Bend.

Sightseeing Highlights

▲**Shaniko**—With a population of 25, Shaniko is Oregon's best-known ghost town. Its name is an Indianization of the surname of its founder, August Scherneckau. In 1900, the arrival of a railroad spur line caused Shaniko to boom as "The Wool Shipping Capital of the World" for ten years before a new railroad route bypassed it. Today, Shaniko's Old West buildings wear fresh coats of paint, and its past glories have been augmented by a church, which was actually a schoolhouse moved here from another ghost town, and a fictitious "Boot Hill" (Shaniko had neither a church nor a cemetery of its own). Several old buildings house museum displays, and a large collection of carriages and buckboards covers a vacant lot near the town center. The historic Shaniko Hotel rents rooms for about $60 a night.

Antelope—Here's a different kind of ghost town. This tiny ranching village (pop. 45) gained national notoriety in the early 1980s, when Bhagwan Sri Rajneesh moved here. The guru originally picked the location, about as far as one can live from modern mainstream civilization, for the quiet, peace, and spiritual freedom he hoped to find there, but soon his 100-square-mile ranch about 18 miles outside town was occupied by thousands of his followers. What's more, 100,000 visitors a year were flocking to see the social and agricultural miracles he had worked there, as well as new boutiques, restaurants, and even a disco. Hopelessly outnumbered, longtime Antelope residents shouted their outrage far and wide. The final indignity came when "Rajneeshees" overwhelmingly voted to change the town's name from Antelope to Rajneesh. The uproar attracted the attention of the federal government, which sent the IRS (rather than the cavalry) galloping to the rescue upon discovering that the guru hadn't paid taxes on Rajneeshpuram's tourist income. Bhagwan Sri Rajneesh was deported to India, his followers scattered, the town's old name was restored, and once again its residents are only outnumbered by pronghorn antelope. *Sic transit gloria mundi.*

▲**John Day Fossil Beds: Clarno Unit**—The least-known of several widely scattered units that comprise John Day Fossil Beds National Monument, Clarno is also the oldest. Found here are fossils from 40 million years ago, when the Cascade Mountains had not yet formed and this area was a subtropical rain forest. Animals whose petrified skeletons have been unearthed at Clarno include tapirs, ancestral horses, primitive rhinoceroses, and other massive vegetarians that have no modern counterparts. While early mammals are more fascinating to laymen, Clarno holds special interest for paleontologists because of the many fossilized nuts, fruits, and seeds that have been discovered here, including prehistoric coconuts and avocados. Two walking trails that begin at the base of the eroded palisades lead you past plant fossil exhibits. Each trail is only a quarter-mile long, and you can walk them both in under an hour.

▲**Fossil Museum**—The town of Fossil has a free local museum of curiosities gathered from around Wheeler County. Like a big, cluttered, slightly dingy antique store without price tags, this museum has eccentric, down-home charm. On display are many items you won't find elsewhere, such as saloon gambling tables, an albino porcupine, a two-headed lamb, a petrified turtle, the only wolverine ever seen (and shot) in the county, and the original city limits sign from Rajneesh, Oregon. Hours are usually about 10:00 a.m. to 4:00 or 4:30 p.m. more or less, most days.

▲▲▲**John Day Fossil Beds National Monument**— From 65 million to 25 million years ago, the John Day region was subtropical forest inhabited by a wide variety of prehistoric mammals. Massive volcanic eruptions buried vast areas in ash, and torrential rains turned the ash to mud, preserving the remains of animals and plants for thousands of millennia—until the late nineteenth century.

In the 1860s this colorful but hostile desert, which remains largely uninhabited, gained international fame. Charles Darwin's recently published *On the Origin of Species* had stirred up the biggest scientific controversy since the notion that the earth might not be flat, and evolution advocates desperately needed fossil evidence to prove their case. When a cavalry troop passing through this desolate area found some fossilized bones and teeth in the sand, the news touched off the academic equivalent of a gold rush, as expeditions from Yale, the University of Pennsylvania, Princeton, and the University of California raced by wagon to scour the desert for signs of prehistoric wildlife. Enduring a harsh climate and harassment by unfriendly Indians, as well as theft and sabotage by competing scientific teams, early paleontologists shipped hundreds of crates of fossils back to eastern museums and changed forever humanity's understanding of the world.

Today the ancestry of modern flora and fauna is well known. Most of us, when we were schoolchildren, stared in wonder at museum exhibits or picture books depicting strange jungle beasts such as saber-toothed tigers, tiny horses, and giant pigs. Yet pictures are one thing; seeing the physical proof, still in the spots where it has lain hidden since long before the dawn of humanity, is quite another. Take time to explore the various units of John Day Fossil Beds, and open your mind to a strange lost world surpassing any in science fiction.

Blue Basin Unit—Although it doesn't appear on most road maps, this small area just north of the Sheep Rock Unit is the most fascinating of the John Day Fossil Beds districts open to the public. The ground here is entirely turquoise blue, and minerals stain the water in the small creek bright green. A half-mile walk into the canyon on the Island in Time Trail, through a landscape so unfamiliar it feels like another planet, takes you past fossilized turtles, saber-toothed cats, oreodonts, and miniature horses. The original fossils are now in museums, but cast reproductions have been placed where they were found. For a longer hike, take the 2-mile Blue Basin Overlook Trail to the top of the ridge for a spectacular view of the area. As you can see, fossils are only exposed when the steep banks erode with rain and wind, so a new one might appear at any time. If you spot one, do not touch it! These fossil skeletons are very fragile and of great scientific value. Immediately report any finds to the rangers at Cant Ranch.

Cant Ranch Visitor Center—The main John Day Fossil Beds Visitor Center is in a 1920s ranch house on the Sheep Rock Unit of the national monument, a few miles south of Blue Basin. (There is a second visitor center in the town of John Day, 38 miles to the east and not included in this itinerary.) The first floor of the main ranch house contains two rooms of interpretive exhibits, an information desk, and an antique-filled living room from the days when it was a private residence. The second floor is where the park rangers live. They divide their time between answering tourist questions, checking out reports of new fossil finds, feeding the livestock, and fixing the roof. Some of the ranch outbuildings house historical exhibits about early paleontologists and a laboratory where you can sometimes watch technicians preparing fossils for display. Other outbuildings shelter sheep.

Painted Hills Unit—Fossils found here are of tree leaves, not animals. You can see some along the quarter-mile Leaf Fossil Hills Trail, though you get a better look at more of them at the Cant Ranch Visitor Center. The real reason to take this side trip 6 miles from the main highway is the scenery: the bold yellow and red striped hills are the brightest-colored bit of painted desert I've seen anywhere in the American West. The best views are from the 1-mile Carroll Rim Trail and the half-mile Painted Hills Overlook Trail.

Camping
The most accessible of the many campgrounds in the Bend area is **Tumalo State Park**, 5 miles northwest of town on US 20 where the highway crosses the Deschutes River, with 68 tent sites and 20 RV sites with hookups, open mid-April through October. Fees are $6 for most sites, $8 for sites with hookups.

The national forest west and south of Bend is full of campgrounds. The best are found at **Newberry Crater**, a little under an hour's drive south of Bend. Along the way are two other small campgrounds you might check out: **Bessen Camp** (about 18 miles south of town on US 97, turn right on Forest Road 40 and go about 2 miles); and **Big River Campground** (2 miles farther south on US 97, take Forest Road 42 on your right). About 2 more miles south on US 97 (22 miles from Bend) is the turnoff on the left to Newberry Crater. Fifteen miles east on this road, you'll enter the crater and find six road-accessible campgrounds totaling more than 300 units, as well as two small hikers-only lakeshore campgrounds. The crater, laced with hiking trails, is endlessly fascinating. If you camp at Newberry Crater tonight, you can visit the Lava Lands sightseeing highlights described in Day 15 on your return trip to Bend tomorrow morning, eat brunch in town, then head back south on the Cascade Lakes Highway. West of Bend on the Cascade Lakes Highway (see the Day 15 travel route), within about 30 miles of town, are lakeside campgrounds at **Todd Lake**, **Devil's Lake**, **Soda Creek**, and **Elk Lake**. None have RV hookups or drinking water.

These are only a sampling of the approximately 80 national forest campgrounds in the area (many of which are far off the highway on unpaved roads). You can get a complete list from the Deschutes National Forest ranger station at 1230 NE Third Street (US 97), Bend, OR 97701, (503) 388-5664.

Lodging

Motels seem to be the main industry in Bend. You won't need reservations. In general, well-furnished, attractive, modern motels in the $50 to $60 price range are along the highway on the north side of town, while older ma-and-pa motels on the south side of town have suffered from the booming competition, resulting in lower rates—typically in the $40 range—for adequate roadside accommodations. Two small (two-unit) B&Bs, for which you need reservations, are near Drake Park and Mirror Pond on the east side of town, in much quieter and more natural settings than any of the motels. They are **Lara House** at 640 NW Congress, (503) 388-4604, about $60; and **Mirror Pond House**, 1054 NW Harmon, (503) 389-1680, about $75. In addition, there are many ski lodge and dude ranch resorts within an hour's drive of Bend—not worth the price if all you want is a place to sleep tonight but interesting options if you plan to spend enough extra time in the area to take advantage of the fishing, boating, and horseback riding possibilities. A complete listing is available from the Bend Chamber of Commerce, 164 NW Hawthorne Avenue, Bend, OR 97701, (503) 382-3221.

At Newberry Crater, an hour south of Bend (see tomorrow's Sightseeing Highlights), **Pauline Lake Resort** has a rustic lodge and log cabins with kitchens. Rates vary from $40 to $100, depending on the unit and the time of year. Call (503) 536-2240 for details and reservations.

Food

Restaurants in Bend outnumber the motels. Virtually every famous-name fast-food franchise has a location here. So do some less-familiar chain restaurants, such as **El Crab Catcher** (389-2722), serving rather expensive seafood at the Inn of the Seventh Mountain out on the Cascade Lakes Highway; it's a spin-off from the restaurant of the same name on the Hawaiian island of Maui. **Le Bistro**, in Bend at 1203 NE Third, 389-7274, is a very good and accordingly high-priced French restaurant in a converted church. Hours are 5:30 to 10:00 p.m., closed Monday. More moderately priced is **Giuseppe's Ristorante**, downtown at 932 NW Bond Street, 389-8899. Outstanding Italian dishes include 17 pasta entrées. Hours are from 5:00 to 9:30 p.m. weekdays, 5:00 to 10:00 p.m. Friday and Saturday, 5:00 to 9:00 p.m. Sunday. Also affordable is **Mexicali Rose**, 301 NW Franklin, 389-0149, serving traditional Mexican food for lunch (weekdays only) 11:30 a.m. to 2:30 p.m. and dinner nightly from 5:00 to 9:30 p.m., until 10:00 p.m. on Friday and Saturday. Last but not least, **Jake's Truck Stop** at the south end of town serves big, inexpensive breakfasts.

LAVA LANDS AND CASCADE LAKES

In Lava Lands, a cluster of unique national forest scenic areas, you can drive to the top of a lava cone, see a lava cave, and wander through a lava cast forest. Afterward, the scenic Cascade Lakes Highway takes you south through the mountains to Crater Lake, site of the biggest bang in Oregon's volcanic history and now the deepest lake in the United States.

Suggested Schedule

(Note: If you camped at Newberry Crater last night, reverse the order of the first three sightseeing highlights on this schedule.)

8:00 a.m.	Drive up Lava Butte.
9:00 a.m.	Visit Lava River Cave.
10:30 a.m.	Visit the Lava Cast Forest.
12:00 noon	Visit the Oregon High Desert Museum or Newberry Crater.
1:00 p.m.	Lunch in Bend.
2:00 p.m.	Drive the Cascade Lakes Highway.
4:00 p.m.	Returning to US 97, drive to Crater Lake.
5:00 p.m.	Arrive at Crater Lake.

Travel Route: Bend to Crater Lake via Cascade Lakes Highway (141 miles, summer only) or US 97 (139 miles)

The Oregon High Desert Museum and the various Lava Lands points of interest are all near US 97 south of Bend. Drive 11 miles south of town to reach Lava Lands Visitor Center, on your right, where the road up Lava Butte begins. One mile farther south, on the opposite side of the road, is Lava River Cave. Two more miles on US 97 will bring you to the turnoff on your left to the Lava Cast Forest. I suggest visiting the Oregon High Desert Museum (7 miles south of Bend) on your way back from Lava Lands to Bend. The museum does not open until 9:00 a.m.

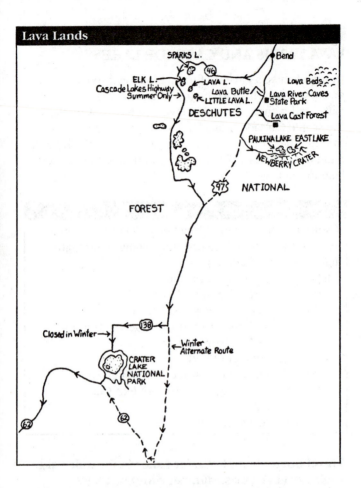

Lava Lands

After lunch in Bend, follow Highway 46 (some signs call it Century Drive, others Cascade Lakes Highway) west from the center of town into Deschutes National Forest. After 25 miles, you'll come to a wayside on the slope of Bachelor Butte, affording a magnificent view of the Three Sisters volcanoes. Just beyond the wayside is Dutchman Flat, a small expanse of pumice desert. The next 50 miles, perhaps the most scenic stretch of road on the east side of the Cascades, provide access to a dozen beautiful lakes. Devil's Lake and Elk Lake are right by the roadside. Pause for a look at Devil's Rock Pile, near Devil's Lake: astronaut

James Irwin, who trained for his lunar expedition in central Oregon during the late 1960s, carried a rock from here to the moon and left it in exchange for the moon rocks his team brought back to earth.

From the main highway, well-marked side roads can take you back to Hosmer Lake (shallow, crystal-clear, and stocked with Atlantic salmon, perfect for fish-watching), Little Lava Lake (the spring-fed headwaters of the Deschutes River) or Cultus Lake (the best for swimming). Osprey Point, on Crane Prairie Reservoir, is reached by an easy nature trail from the parking area. The eagle-like American osprey (fishhawk), once considered a vanishing species in the United States, is now quite common around this reservoir, and if you visit between April and October you may see one of these birds diving from hundreds of feet in the air to grab a fish in its razor-sharp talons.

Continue south on the Cascade Lakes Highway as far as you can go, and you'll reach a T-intersection. Turn left (east), and another 8 miles will bring you back to US 97. Proceed south on US 97 for 28 miles and turn right (west) on Highway 138. Fifteen more miles will bring you to the north gate of Crater Lake National Park.

Off-season alternate route: Both the Cascade Lakes Highway and Crater Lake's north gate are closed by snow until late spring. Early-season travelers can get from Bend to Crater Lake only by driving directly south on US 97 for 110 miles, then turning back northwest on Highway 62 for 29 miles to the Crater Lake south gate. This route is much faster than the Cascade Lakes Highway but not nearly as scenic.

Sightseeing Highlights
▲▲**Lava Lands Visitors Center/Lava Butte**—Lava Lands, which includes Lava Butte, Lava River Cave, Lava Cast Forest, and Newberry Crater, is a de facto park operated by the U.S. Forest Service in Deschutes National Forest. Admission is free to all Lava Lands points of interest. The visitor center, at the foot of Lava Butte, features several large, automated dioramas showing the volcanic and human history of the area, including one where you

can watch a model of Mount Mazama explode and collapse to become Crater Lake. Two short nature trails leave from the visitor center, taking you across a lava flow and through a pine forest. Drive up the dizzying spiral road to the summit of Lava Butte, a small, perfectly cone-shaped volcano, where a quarter-mile trail leads around the crater, commanding panoramic views of the Lava Lands area, the Three Sisters, Mount Bachelor, and more distant peaks of the Cascades.

▲**Benham Falls**—Six miles west on the wide unpaved forest road that starts near the Lava Lands Visitors Center is a day-use fishing and picnic area with the biggest trees in the woods. The local lumber company, which logged the forest around Bend so thoroughly from 1916 to the 1940s that they finally declared it worthless and donated the land to the forest service for rehabilitation, left this stand of tall ponderosa intact because it was the site of their annual company picnic. They used to bring 2,000 employees and their families out here from Bend each year on railroad flatcars for the picnic. Cross the bridge and take an easy walk along the old railroad bed, now trackless and blocked from vehicle traffic, to the falls overlook. As you stroll beside the lazy Deschutes River, imagine what it would be like to glide gently along in a canoe. Minutes later, your daydream will turn into a classic movie heart-stopper: you'll feel like Hepburn and Bogart in *The African Queen*, or Monroe and Mitchum in *River of No Return*, as the placid river rounds a bend and suddenly plunges into a spectacular series of whitewater cataracts.

▲▲**Lava River Cave**—A self-guided, 1-hour, 1¼-mile walk takes you through the longest known uncollapsed lava tube in Oregon (about 6,700 feet, the last 1,500 feet of which are closed to the public because of dangerous loose rocks). The tunnel is as much as 58 feet high and 50 feet wide in some places, while elsewhere the ceiling is as low as 5½ feet. The sand that covers most of the cave floor is from the Mount Mazama (Crater Lake) eruption. There is no electric lighting; bring a flashlight, or, in summer months only, rent a lantern at the cave entrance.

▲▲**Lava Cast Forest**—During an eruption from Newberry Volcano about 6,000 years ago, molten lava oozed slowly through a ponderosa pine forest, forming a hard coating around each tree. Standing trees and fallen logs, some in piles, left the unique molded impressions you see today along the 1-mile trail.

▲**Oregon High Desert Museum**—The assortment of exhibits at this indoor-outdoor museum ranges from Lewis and Clark memorabilia and forestry displays to a settler's cabin, an Indian wickiup shelter, and a chuckwagon where frontier cooking is demonstrated. Live animal exhibits, including otters and birds of prey, are enlivened as human handlers give frequent presentations. This could be your chance of a lifetime to watch someone cuddle a porcupine. The museum is open daily from 9:00 a.m. to 5:00 p.m. Admission is $5.50 for adults, $5 for senior citizens, $2.75 for children ages 6 to 12.

▲**Newberry Crater**—Less than an hour's drive south of Bend, camp and explore this collapsed crater of the largest ice-age volcano in Oregon. Twenty-five miles across, Newberry Crater is larger than Crater Lake, though not as deep, and contains two lakes separated by an area of recent eruptions. Within the crater are 68 miles of hiking trails. The crater's most unusual feature is a massive flow of obsidian (shiny black volcanic glass) that extends from the main road nearly to the south rim. For many centuries, Indians came here to gather obsidian for tools and weapons, and they left chipped fragments that are often found along the shores of both lakes. To reach Newberry Crater, continue for 22 miles south of Bend on US 97 and turn left on the paved road that takes you 15 miles east to the crater.

Camping
Mazama Campground at Crater Lake National Park, near the south entrance gate, has 198 campsites at $8 each. The only other camping in the park is at **Lost Creek** on the road to the Pinnacles, with 12 primitive sites, tents only, free. Both campgrounds are only open from the 4th of July through September.

If you can't find a campsite in the national park, national forest campgrounds are small but numerous to the west of the park. From the north entrance gate, drive 7 miles north to **Diamond Lake** and look for campsites around the lake; if you don't find one to your liking there, follow Highway 230 west from the south end of the lake, and after about 12 miles you'll see the first of a half-dozen campgrounds between there and Union Creek. If you're leaving the park by the south entrance, drive 16 miles west to Union Creek and check out the three camp-grounds nearby; turn north on Highway 30 toward Dia-mond Lake and you'll find more. Some of these national forest campgrounds open in late May, others not until July; some close by mid-September, others stay open through October.

Food and Lodging

Crater Lake Lodge on the south rim at Rim Village has 80 guest rooms and a few rustic cabins. Rates start at about $65. The lodge is open from early June through September 15. Make reservations far in advance by writing to Crater Lake Lodge Company, P.O. Box 97, Crater Lake, OR 97604, or by calling (503) 594-2511. The lodge has a restaurant and a cafeteria.

While the location is incomparable at Crater Lake Lodge, in some ways I prefer **Union Creek Resort**, 16 miles west of the Crater Lake south entrance gate on Highway 230. It's smaller and friendlier, rates are much lower, reservations are usually easier to get on short notice, and it's open all year. Rustic cabins start at about $60 a night, rooms in the lodge (all with shared bath) about $45. This early-1900s "resort," on the National Register of Historic Places, doesn't have any of the usual resort amenities like a swimming pool, a golf course, or tennis courts. It does have a game room with a big stone fireplace, a country grocery store, a little café that's famous for its homemade huckleberry pies, a creek running through the yard, and nothing but forest all around for miles and miles and miles. Write to Union Creek Resort, Prospect, OR 97536, or call (503) 560-3565.

CRATER LAKE NATIONAL PARK

Here it is: the most awe-inspiring extinct volcano in the national park system. Later, for a complete change of pace, drive to Ashland and enjoy an evening at the theater—sixteenth-century style.

Suggested Schedule

9:00 a.m.	Drive to Rim Village Visitors Center.
9:30 a.m.	See the visitors center.
10:00 a.m.	Explore Crater Lake. Drive the Rim Road. Hike down to the lakeshore, or take a tour boat to Wizard Island and explore the island on foot.
4:00 p.m.	Leave for Ashland.
6:00 p.m.	Arrive in Ashland. Check into your lodgings and eat dinner.
8:30 p.m.	Shakespeare under the stars at the Elizabethan Stage.

Crater Lake National Park

As early as the tenth century B.C., ancestors of the Klamath Indians lived in the shadow of 12,000-foot Mount Mazama, the southernmost major volcano in the Cascade Range, then about the same height as Mount Adams is today. According to legends that have survived into historical times, the Indians believed that Mazama's fiery eruptions were battles between two gods. In 4860 B.C., the gods' "war" reached a climax, when the mountain exploded with a force 42 times that of Mount St. Helens' 1980 eruption, hurling rock and ash over 5,000 square miles of what are now eight states and three Canadian provinces. The volcano collapsed, leaving a crater 6 miles across, which filled with water to a depth of 1,932 feet and created the deepest lake in the United States.

So sacred was Crater Lake to Native Americans that shamans forbade their people from going there. Indians never mentioned the place to white pioneers, who explored the area for fifty years before "discovering"

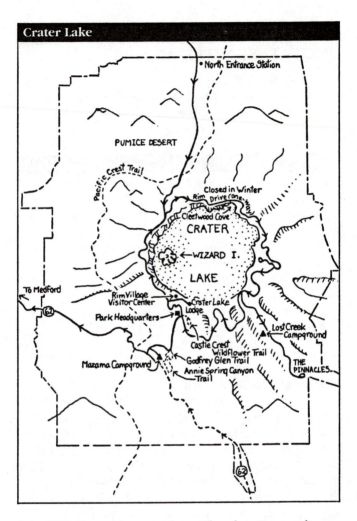

Crater Lake

it in 1853. Forty-nine years later, Theodore Roosevelt declared Crater Lake the United States' sixth national park.

The volcano under Crater Lake has been dormant for about a thousand years. However, in August 1987, scientists discovered an active thermal vent on the lake bottom, which they are now studying with minisubmarines and remote-control underwater video cameras.

Deep snow keeps most roads in the park closed until July and closes them again in October. If you are visiting at any time except July, August, and September, the only road you can drive will be the one from the south entrance to park headquarters at Rim Village. The other park roads are used off-season for cross-country skiing, and rangers lead snowshoe trips on weekend afternoons from December through May. A complete circuit of the rim on skis takes about three days.

During the short summer season, the 33-mile drive around the Crater Rim Road lets you view the lake from every angle. The longest segment of the road, along the east side of the lake, is one-way from the north gate road to Rim Village and the visitor center at the south gate road—so no matter where you start, drive in a clockwise direction.

The only way to hike down to the lake is on Cleetwood Trail, a steep 1-mile descent from the picnic area above Cleetwood Cove to the boat landing. From there, a narrated boat tour (daily, between 9:00 a.m. and 3:00 p.m., July and August only, $10 for adults, $5.50 for children 12 and under) takes you counterclockwise along the shore to Wizard Island, the volcanic cone that rises out of the lake near the west shore. The tour takes two hours, including a short stop on the island; catch a morning trip and you can stay on the island to hike the mile-long trail that spirals to the top of the cone, then board a midafternoon tour boat for the return trip. Other short hikes in the park include the easy half-mile Castle Crest Wildflower Trail, which starts near the park headquarters, the 1½-mile Godfrey Glen Trail 2 miles down the south gate road, and the 1¾-mile Annie Spring Canyon Trail from Mazama Canyon near the south gate. For a longer hike, go as far as you want on the Pacific Crest Trail, which intersects the north gate road and crosses the Pumice Desert.

Travel Route: Crater Lake to Ashland (89 miles)

From the south gate of Crater Lake, take Highway 62 west bound for 72 miles to Medford, where you join Interstate 5. Take the interstate southbound for 17 miles to Ashland.

Ashland: The Oregon Shakespeare Festival

"Men are merriest when they are from home" (*Henry V,* Act I). The mountains of southwestern Oregon are farther from Merry Old England than were dreamt of in Shakespeare's philosophy. Yet here you'll find the nation's finest performances of his plays. The Oregon Shakespeare Festival, the oldest and largest in the United States, dates back to 1935 and plays to 300,000 people each year. In 1983, the festival won a Tony Award, the theater equivalent of the Oscar.

The Oregon Shakespeare Festival runs from mid-February through the end of October, with performances daily except Mondays. However, the Elizabethan Stage (an exact reproduction of London's circa 1600 Fortune Theatre), where Shakespeare's plays are presented outdoors, as when they were first performed, only operates from mid-June through September. The festival also includes indoor performances at the nearby Agnes Bowmer Theatre and the more intimate Black Swan Theater, but most of the plays performed in the indoor theaters are not Shakespearean. Instead, they range from modern classics by Ibsen, O'Neill, and Pirandello to premieres of works by contemporary playwrights.

Performances on the Elizabethan Stage begin at 8:30 p.m. Old English dances are performed outside the theater before the play. Ticket prices range from $16 to $24. For the current season's schedule and ticket ordering information, write: Oregon Shakespeare Festival, Box 158, Ashland, OR 97520. To be on the safe side, you should order tickets several months in advance. If you didn't, call the box office at (503) 482-4331 to inquire about last-minute ticket availability.

Lodging

Ashland, in addition to its many motels, has the largest selection of B&B inns in Oregon. A few of the nearly three dozen possibilities are **The Morical House**, an elegantly restored 1880s home at 668 North Main, Ashland, OR 97520, (503) 482-9296, $80 to $112; **Oak Street Station Bed & Breakfast**, a Queen Anne home at 239 Oak Street, (503) 482-1726, $75 to $85; the **Queen Anne**, 125 North Main Street, (503) 482-0220, $75 to $90; and the quietly luxurious **Romeo Inn**, 295 Idaho, (503) 488-0884, starting at $115. For a complete listing of Ashland B&Bs, contact the Ashland Chamber of Commerce, P.O. Box 606, Ashland, OR 97520, (503) 482-3486.

The Columbia Hotel, 262 E. Main, (503) 482-3726, is a small European-style historic hotel just a block from the theaters. Rates start under $50. The **Ashland Hostel** at 150 North Main, (503) 482-9217, offers dormitory beds at just $9.50 a night for AYH members.

Two miles north of town on Highway 99, you can rent a rustic cabin with kitchen facilities for as little as $40 a night and enjoy the 50-by-100-foot hot mineral pool at **Jackson Hot Springs**, 2235 Highway 99 North, (503) 482-3776. Camping is also available there.

Food

My favorite Ashland restaurant is **Omar's** at the intersection of Siskiyou Boulevard and Highway 66; call 482-1281 for reservations. Since it opened in 1946, Omar's has been known for its outstanding steak and seafood selections, reasonably priced. Try the "Toad in the Hole" (sounds ghastly but tastes great and doesn't actually involve eating an amphibian), or, if you are less adventurous, the Dijon chicken.

Also in Ashland, an intimate, uncompromisingly romantic French restaurant is the **Chateaulin** at 50 East Main, open daily, hours vary seasonally, expensive, reservations required, 482-2264. More moderate in price, but at least as unusual, is the **Immigrant**, 19 First Street, serving authentic Afghani dinners from 5:00 to 8:00 p.m. during the festival season, 482-2547. You'll find inexpensive fare and a deck overlooking the creek at the **Greenleaf Delicatessen**, 49 North Main, open Monday 9:00 a.m. to 3:00 p.m., Tuesday through Sunday 9:00 a.m. to 8:00 p.m., 482-2808. For an Ashland dining experience as outrageous as its name, check out the **Bushes Rock & Roll Burger Bar** (no relation to George) at 1474 Siskiyou Boulevard, where amid the din of video games you can sink your teeth into what they claim is the largest flame-broiled hamburger in the world.

ASHLAND TO THE COAST

On your way to the Pacific coast, take time to see Oregon's largest cave and some of California's tallest trees.

Suggested Schedule

10:00 a.m.	Backstage tour.
12:00 noon	Lunch.
1:00 p.m.	Leave Ashland and drive to Oregon Caves.
3:00 p.m.	Tour Oregon Caves National Monument.
4:30 p.m.	Drive to Jedediah Smith Redwoods State Park. Camp there.

Travel Route: Ashland to Crescent City via Oregon Caves (142 miles)

From Ashland, return north on Interstate 5 for 48 miles to the second Grants Pass exit. Follow US 199 for 31 miles to the turnoff at Cave Junction for Oregon Caves National Monument, a 20-mile drive each way.

Returning to US 199, drive south 50 miles to Jedediah Smith Redwoods State Park and the intersection with US 101. (Crescent City, a good place to find a motel, is 4 miles farther on the same highway.)

Sightseeing Highlights

▲▲**Oregon Shakespeare Festival Backstage Tour**—This 2-hour tour is almost better than the plays themselves. A guide brimming with historical information and gossip will meet you at the Black Swan and lead you behind the scenes of the Elizabethan Stage to show you stagehands at work, dressing rooms, and the green room, where actors relax when they're not on stage. You can also see and handle costumes and props such as broadswords and severed heads. The tour costs $7.50. It starts promptly at 10:00 a.m. Reservations are required; call (503) 482-4331. There are no tours on Mondays.

▲▲**Oregon Caves National Monument**—This cave

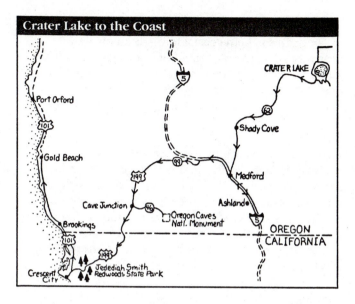

Crater Lake to the Coast

(there's only one, despite the name) is Oregon's largest and, as far as I've been able to determine, the largest on the West Coast. At the end of a narrow, winding paved road, which climbs to 4,020 feet in elevation, the cave penetrates an outcropping of solid marble to a series of large rooms dripping with stalactites, flowstone curtains, and columns. Visitors can enter the cave only on 75-minute guided tours offered by the Oregon Caves Company, a private concessioner. Frequent tours run daily from early June through Labor Day 8:00 a.m. to 7:00 p.m., May and September from 9:00 a.m. to 5:00 p.m., and the rest of the year at 10:30 a.m. and 12:30, 2:00, and 3:30 p.m. only. The cost of the tour is $6.75 for adults, $3.75 for children ages 6 to 11. Children under 6 years old are not allowed on the tour, but child care is available for $3 per child.

▲▲**Jedediah Smith Redwoods State Park**—This California state park is on the only direct route from inland Oregon to the south Oregon coast. Adjacent to Redwood National Park, it preserves 18 memorial redwood stands along the Smith River, including the 5,000-acre National Tribute Grove. The park's largest tree is 20 feet in diameter and 340 feet tall.

Redwood trees like these once grew throughout much of Oregon's southern coastal forest, but now they're nearly all gone. (A small stand of redwoods can still be found in Oregon at Loeb State Park, where there is also one of the best surviving myrtlewood groves, about 8 miles inland from Brookings on Chetco River Road.)

Camping

There is a 108-site campground at **Jedediah Smith Redwoods State Park**, $10, open all year. Reservations are accepted; call (800) 444-7275 in California. California state park reservations can be a problem on short notice. First-come, first-served camping can be found along US 199 at several national forest campgrounds—**Cedar Rustic, Patrick Creek, Grassy Flat**, and **Panther Flat**, all within 10 miles east of Gasquet.

Lodging

Crescent City has a reasonable selection of motels. **Curley Redwood Lodge**, a motel that the owners boast was built entirely from a single redwood tree, is at 701 Redwood Highway South, (707) 464-2137. Rates start around $60 a night.

A more interesting alternative is to spend the night in **Oregon Caves Château** at the national monument. Rooms at this rustic 1934 lodge cost $66. A creek runs right through the dining room. For reservations, write Oregon Caves Château, P.O. Box 128, Cave Junction, OR 97523, or call (503) 592-3400. Open from Memorial Day to Labor Day only.

Near Oregon Caves, at 250 Robinson in Cave Junction, dormitory accommodations are available in the AYH-affiliated **Fordson Home Hostel**. Reservations are essential; call (503) 592-3203.

Helpful Hint

This book connects with Day 19 of Roger Rapoport's *2 to 22 Days in California* (Santa Fe, N.M.: John Muir Publications, 1993) at Crescent City. Californians visiting Oregon and Washington, Northwesterners traveling to California, and anyone wishing to enjoy the ultimate 44-day round-trip tour of Pacific Coast states should own a copy of Roger's book as a companion to this one.

SOUTHERN OREGON COAST

US 101 parallels the coast for 1,556 miles from Los Angeles, California, north to Port Angeles, Washington, and then swings south again to Olympia. Ahead, you have a 346-mile drive up the Oregon coast and another 286 miles around the Olympic Peninsula to return to the Seattle area. That's an average of just 126 miles per day for the next five days, but the many breathtaking view points and inviting beaches will make you long for twice as much time to explore.

Suggested Schedule

8:30 a.m.	Leave Crescent City, drive north to Gold Beach.
10:00 a.m.	Continue north to Bandon.
11:30 a.m.	Drive to Cape Arago.
12:30 p.m.	Picnic at Cape Arago.
1:30 p.m.	Visit Shore Acres.
2:30 p.m.	Drive to Coos Bay.
3:00 p.m.	Drive to Dunes Overlook.
4:00 p.m.	Hike the dunes.
5:30 p.m.	Camp at one of the Siltcoos camp-grounds or Honeyman State Park, or stay at a motel in Florence.

Travel Route: Crescent City, California, to Honeyman State Park, Oregon (140 miles)

Heading north on US 101 from Crescent City, you will drive 51 miles to Gold Beach. Another 55 miles, and you'll be in Bandon.

The driving distance on US 101 from Bandon north to the campgrounds at Siltcoos Lake, Dunes, and Beach is 64 miles, and you have all afternoon to get there. Take the scenic route. Either of two turnoffs to the left, about 5 miles and 10 miles north of Bandon, will take you past the South Slough Estuarine Sanctuary, then to the village of Charleston, where a dead-end road takes you to Sunset Bay, Shore Acres, and Cape Arago.

Returning through Charleston, keep going straight into Coos Bay, where you'll find your way back onto US 101. From there north to the campgrounds, the Oregon Dunes National Recreation Area lies between you and the ocean on your left, while on your right is a series of lakes.

Sightseeing Highlights

Oregon's coast is 350 miles of practically continuous parks. A unique state law makes all seashore below the mean high tide mark public land, and 67 state parks and waysides along US 101, as well as a 45-mile-long national recreation area, give access to the beaches and rocky shores practically everywhere. I've pared the list of Oregon coast scenic spots down to the "must sees" plus a few less-known personal favorites. Despite such ruthless selectivity, today's and tomorrow's Sightseeing Highlights include more spectacular scenery and special places than any traveler could hope to visit in just two days. Here they are. Take your pick.

▲**Brookings**—Horticulture is a major industry in Brookings, where 90 percent of all the lilies sold commercially in the United States are grown. Azalea State Park, in town, is a botanical wonderland—and a must see if you're passing through in May, when the azaleas bloom. In April, Brookings's annual Driftwood Show brings together serious beachcombers. North of town, Harris Beach State Park and Samuel H. Boardman State Park (the latter named after the "Father of the Oregon State Park System") provide access to miles of coastline where you can collect your own souvenir driftwood. Particularly attractive stops include Whalehead Beach, less than a quarter-mile from the turnoff 6 miles north of Brookings, where an offshore rock appears to spout like a whale; Indian Sands Trail, about a mile north of Whalehead Beach, a short, steep hike through forests and fields of flowers to the sea; Natural Bridge, 2 miles north of Indian Sands, a fascinating, photogenic view point of an island linked to the mainland by a rock span; and Arch Rock, about a half mile from the turnoff 3 miles north of the Natural Bridge Viewpoint, an unusual formation in a sheer cliff seascape.

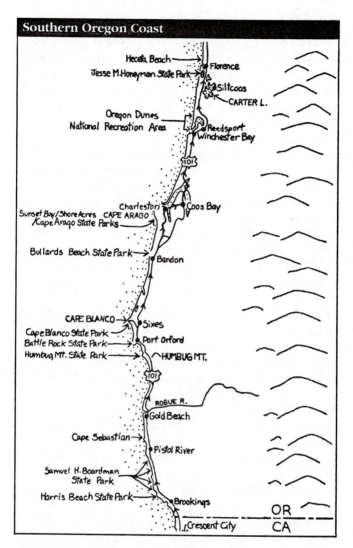

Southern Oregon Coast

Heceta Beach → ● Florence
Jesse M. Honeyman State Park →
● Siltcoos
← CARTER L.
Oregon Dunes
National Recreation Area
● Reedsport
Winchester Bay
101
Charleston ● Coos Bay
Sunset Bay/Shore Acres
/Cape Arago State Parks
CAPE ARAGO
Bullards Beach State Park → ● Bandon
CAPE BLANCO → ● Sixes
Cape Blanco State Park
Battle Rock State Park → Port Orford
Humbug Mt. State Park → HUMBUG MT.
101
ROGUE R.
● Gold Beach
Cape Sebastian →
● Pistol River
Samuel H. Boardman
State Park
Harris Beach State Park → ● Brookings
OR
Crescent City
CA

▲**Cape Sebastian**—About 23 miles north of Brookings and 6 miles south of Gold Beach, turn off on a steep road up to the top of a 700-foot cliff that commands perhaps the finest view to be found on the southern Oregon coast.
▲**Gold Beach**—This resort community's main attraction is jet-boat touring on the Rogue River, one of only 13 federally designated Wild and Scenic Rivers in the United

States. No time has been set aside in this 22-day itinerary for the jet-boat trip, but if you have a spare day, here's a great way to spend it. The hydrojet boats carry up to 49 passengers, shoulder-to-shoulder, upriver through virgin forests and rugged canyons teeming with wildlife. You may see black bears, river otters, bald eagles, and beavers. Two-hour, 36-mile round-trips leave at 8:00 or 8:30 a.m. and 2:30 p.m. and cost $20 for adults and $10 for children ages 4 to 11. Longer jetboat trips are also available, as well as 1- to 3-day raft trips. Trips run daily, May through October; inquire about occasional winter trips. Reservations are recommended; in July and August they are essential. For complete information, contact Rogue River Mail Boats, P.O. Box 1165, Gold Beach, OR 97444, (503) 247-7033; Court's at Jot's Resort, P.O. Box J, Gold Beach, OR 97444, (503) 247-6676; or Jerry's Rogue River Jet Boats, P.O. Box 1011, Gold Beach, OR 97444, (503) 247-4571.

▲▲**Humbug Mountain State Park**—Twenty-one miles north of Gold Beach, this park offers the best hiking on the southern Oregon coast—a 3-mile climb to the summit of 1,756-foot Humbug Mountain overlooking the seashore. This is an ambitious half-day hike. For an easier stroll, the beach here—several miles long—is one of the best for beachcombing. Look for agate, driftwood, unusual seashells, and the rarest of seashore treasures, Japanese glass floats.

▲**Battle Rock State Park**—At the south end of Port Orford is the rock where, in 1851, nine would-be settlers retreated from unfriendly Indians. On top of the rock, they awaited a chance to move their colony farther up the coast. Climb to the cluster of pines on top of Battle Rock for the view, and bring binoculars. Sea otters, once nearly extinct, are making a comeback and can sometimes be spotted among the rocks to the south.

▲**Cape Blanco State Park**—The 1870 lighthouse at the westernmost point in Oregon is typical of lighthouses found all along the Oregon coast. It is still in use, and the Coast Guard conducts free tours. Here you'll also find a rare stretch of black sand beach.

▲**Bandon**—The self-proclaimed "Storm-Watching Capital of the World," Bandon has done an admirable job of rebuilding its town center, which was destroyed by fire in the 1930s and long-neglected afterward. The mostly new Old Town houses outstanding gourmet and gift shops. Cranberries and myrtlewood products are local specialties. The biggest local holiday is the Cranberry Festival on the second weekend in September, but the year's most intriguing event is the sand castle sculpture contest held annually on Memorial Day, with stiff competition for cash prizes. If you'd like to participate, call the Bandon Chamber of Commerce at (505) 347-9616, and they'll send you an entry form.

▲**Bullard Beach State Park**—This long, broad beach 3 miles north of Bandon is an ideal place to get sand between your toes and hunt for pretty pebbles. Watch out for equestrians and off-road vehicles, though.

▲▲**South Slough Estuarine Sanctuary**—There's more to the Northwest Coast than beaches, dunes, and rocky headlands. Here you can explore coastal wetlands where fresh water flows into the ocean—or, when the tide is rising, where salt water flows into the estuary. This buffer zone supports abundant and varied wildlife. Thanks to the perseverance of local environmentalists, the 4,400-acre sanctuary at South Slough was the first of 20 wild coastal wetlands to be preserved in its natural state under the federal Coastal Zone Management Act. It is a rookery for great blue herons and also attracts birds that migrate along the Pacific Coast Flyway. Beavers, bald eagles, black-tailed deer, and fish, including trout, salmon, steelhead, sea bass, and shellfish, make their homes here. You can see the whole estuary from the Interpretive Center. A 3-mile Estuary Study Trail descends by loops through the forest, past an abandoned pioneer homestead, to salt marshes, tide flats, and open water. The round-trip takes about 2 hours.

▲**Sunset Bay State Park**—This is the first of three quite different parks on the Cape Arago Highway. From Seven Devils Road, turn left at Winchester; it's 5 miles to the end of the "highway." This small, round, secluded bay framed by forests of Douglas fir takes its name from the fact that it is most beautiful at sunset. The beach is peaceful and picture-perfect any time of day.

▲▲**Shore Acres State Park**—Just down the road from Sunset Bay, these formal gardens were the legacy of lumber baron Louis J. Simpson, who used profits from cutting forests to landscape over 100 acres of rose gardens, Japanese gardens, rhododendrons, and azaleas. His mansion burned to the ground more than 50 years ago, but his gardens remain spectacular under the care of the state park service.

▲▲**Cape Arago State Park**—Buy your picnic lunch in Bandon and eat it here. Secluded picnic tables overlook the sea. Sea lions often bask on the rocks offshore. At low tide, explore the tide pools at any of three coves below. North Cove, the best, largest, and easiest to reach, is a good spot to see sea anemones.

Coos Bay—The return trip along the Cape Arago Highway will bring you into the heart of Coos Bay, the largest town on the Oregon coast and the second-largest U.S. lumber shipping port. The principal sightseeing highlight in town is the Weyerhauser Lumber Mill, US 101 at Newmark Street, 756-5121, which offers free 90-minute tours Monday through Friday, between 10:30 a.m. and 1:30 p.m., mid-June through August. The lumber industry will be a gut-wrenching presence for the next few days as you drive up the Olympic Peninsula. The Coos Bay Sawmill alone churned out 20 billion board-feet of lumber last year. This plant tour will overwhelm you with the harsh reality of where forest products, from your furniture to the pages these words are printed on, actually come from. (Keep reminding yourself, "it's only a renewable resource." If you care about the natural environment, it's okay to cry.) A less traumatic Coos Bay stop is the **Coos Art Museum** at 235 Anderson Avenue, 267-3901, exhibit open Tuesday through Friday 11:00 a.m. to 5:00 p.m., Saturday and Sunday 1:00 to 4:00 p.m. Suggested donation is $2 for adults, $1 for children.

▲▲▲**Oregon Dunes National Recreation Area**—The Oregon Dunes extend north from Coos Bay 45 miles to

Florence. Coastal rocks in this area are sandstone, so over millennia, erosion from ocean waves has deposited prodigious quantities of sand on the beach. At low tide, winds blow the sand inland to create the dunes. Some of the sandpiles are over 500 feet high—taller than those of the Sahara Desert. Neither the ocean nor the largest expanses of open sand are visible from the highway for most of the drive, but short hiking trails can take you across the sand from several waysides along US 101. Take your pick—any of them makes for an ideal 1- to 2-hour hike. Eel Creek Trail and Umpqua Dunes Scenic Area Trail (each ¼ mile to open sand, another 2 miles to the beach) start at Eel Creek Campground, about 13 miles north of Coos Bay. About 11 miles north of the town of Reedsport, where the Oregon Dunes National Recreation Area Headquarters and Information Center is located, Tahkenitch Campground is the trailhead for Tahkenitch Trail (¾ mile through coastal forest to open sand, another mile to the beach). About a mile north of Tahkenitch Campground, at Oregon Dunes Overlook, the Overlook Trail starts at the south viewing platform (1 mile to the beach). Just north of there, the Carter Dunes Trail starts at Carter Lake Campground (¼ mile to open sand, 1¼ miles farther to the beach). On open sand the footpaths are invisible; follow the wooden posts to find your way. While exploring the dunes, wrap your camera in a plastic bag to protect the mechanism from sand.

▲▲**Siltcoos Lake, Dunes, and Beach**—The cluster of campgrounds and paved beach access roads here offer the most varied hiking in the Oregon Dunes area. An estuary creates wetlands among the dunes from the ocean to Siltcoos Lake, Oregon's largest coastal lake, on the east side of US 101. Across US 101 from the main beach access road, the Siltcoos Lake Trail, 2 miles through lush 50-year-old second-growth forest to the lakeshore, is a favorite spot of mushroom hunters; the trail is presently being extended to 3.3 miles. On the west side of the highway along the beach access road, walk the River of No Return Nature Trail (easy ½-mile loop from Lagoon Campground), the Chief Tsiltcoos Trail (1 mile to the beach from the trailhead by the main beach access road west of the Waxmyrtle Campground turnoff), or the Fisherman's Trail (1½ miles along the river from Waxmyrtle Campground to the beach). You can usually see wildlife in the wetlands areas along these trails, especially at sunset Recently on an after-dinner walk on the Chief Tsiltcoos Trail, I watched for half an hour as five fearless beavers swam around the pond, sometimes approaching within five feet of where I stood. Speaking of wildlife, when exploring these trails be sure to wear insect repellent.

▲▲▲**Jessie M. Honeyman State Park**—About 6 miles north on US 101 from the the Siltcoos turnoff is the pride of the Oregon State Parks system. A truly vast campground and meticulous landscaping surround picture-perfect little Cleawox Lake, flanked by high sand dunes that create a big, steeply slanted beach for sunbathers. The lakeshore is usually crowded, and some nature lovers find the carefully shaped shrubbery flanking paved trails a bit too perfect; nevertheless, many Northwesterners cite this as their favorite park on the Oregon coast The campers' grocery store here has a low-priced snack bar. Popular trails lead from the park to the dunes and ocean beach

Camping

Jessie M. Honeyman State Park is generally known as the finest campground in Oregon. It's certainly one of the biggest (382 campsites, second only to the campground at Fort Stevens). Despite its size, reservations are required here between Memorial Day weekend and Labor Day weekend but are not necessary at other times of year. To make a reservation, you must write for a campsite reservation application to Honeyman, 84505 Highway 101, Florence, OR 97439, or call the State Campsite Information Center at (800) 452-5687 within Oregon or (503) 238-7488. When you receive the application, fill it out, and enclose a check for $10 ($7 deposit toward the first night's camping fee plus $3 nonrefundable reservation fee). Mail it directly to Honeyman State Park at the above address. Reservations can't be made by phone; cancellations can. If you cancel before 6:00 p.m. on the reservation date, you'll receive by mail a $7 "rain check" good for camping fees at any Oregon State Park.

In other words, reserving a campsite at Honeyman or any of the 12 other Oregon state parks that require reservations is a big hassle. If you don't have a reservation, you might be able to get a campsite anyway. Campsites that have not been reserved or for which cancellations have been received are assigned on a first-come, first-served basis.

The national forest campgrounds at Siltcoos Lake, Dunes, and Beach, and nearby Carter Lake don't have a reservation system, though they can also fill up early, especially on summer weekends and holidays.

Lodging

The Florence area's largest hotel, and the only one on the ocean, is **Driftwood Shores Surfside Resort**, at 88416 First Avenue, about four miles north of town via Heceta Beach Road, (503) 997-8263. The resort has a beach, a spa, and an indoor pool, and rooms have balconies overlooking the ocean. Rates run $92 June through September, as low as $72 off-season. Another outstanding lodging choice is the **Johnson House**, a Victorian B&B downtown at the corner of First and Maple streets, just a block from the bayfront. Rates range from $60 to $85 in season (mid-June through September), slightly less off-season. For reservations, write to the Johnson House, P.O. Box 1892, Florence, OR 97439, or call (503) 997-8000.

The **Money Saver Motel**, ¾-mile south of Florence at 170 Highway 101, (503) 997-7131, offers rooms starting at $50 in season (June through September), $14 less off-season. You can save more money on one of the small, rustic rooms starting at $44 at the **Park Motel**, 85030 Highway 101, (503) 987-2634.

Florence has no hostel accommodations. You'll find them elsewhere along the coast at the **Sea Star Hostel** in Bandon, (503) 347-9533; the **Sea Gull Hostel** in Coos Bay, (503) 267-6114 (open Memorial Day through Labor Day only); and the **Newport Hostel** in Newport, (503) 265-9816.

Food

Both Bandon and Florence have numerous regional and
specialty food shops in their Old Town areas. Besides
buying picnic food for today, now is a good time to start
stocking up on gourmet groceries for the remainder of
your trip. After you cross back into the state of Washington on Day 20, fine dining or even grocery shopping
opportunities will be quite limited for the rest of the trip.

In Bandon, the **Fish Market** on First Street at the boat
basin sells seafood from the local catch, as well as canned
and smoked fish. Also on First Street, the **Cranberry
Sweets Company** sells various types of candy made from
the region's major fruit product. **Bandon's Cheddar
Cheese** not only sells the cheese but makes it in public
view.

In Florence, **Incredible Edible Oregon** at 1336 Bay
Street has a wide array of regional specialty foods from all
over Oregon. The **Old Sarajevo Bakery** at 185 Maple
Street is a fine little European-style pastry shop.

For dinner in Florence, you'll find outstanding seafood,
especially shellfish, at the **Bridgewater Seafood Restaurant**, 1297 Bay Street, open daily 11:00 a.m. to 9:00
p.m., Friday and Saturday until 10:00 p.m., 997-9405.
Meals here are fairly expensive. More moderately priced
seafood, along with fabulous baked goods, can be found
at the large but tasteful **Windward Inn**, 3757 US 101,
open Tuesday through Sunday from 8:00 a.m. to 9:00
p.m., 997-8243. For breakfast, just-plain-good food at very
reasonable prices is served from 7:00 a.m. to 2:00 p.m. at
Morgan's Country Kitchen, 85020 Highway 101 South,
997-6991.

NORTHERN OREGON COAST

The Oregon coast is a kaleidoscope of booming tourist resorts, quaint old fishing villages, lighthouses, tide pools, broad beaches, seaswept headlands, sea lions, sea anemones, seafood, and Seaside. Evening will find you at the mouth of the Columbia River. (Lewis and Clark slept here.)

Suggested Schedule

8:30 a.m.	Drive to Cape Perpetua.
9:30 a.m.	Visit Cape Perpetua.
10:30 a.m.	Drive to Sea Lion Cave.
11:00 a.m.	Sea Lion Cave.
12:00 noon	Drive to Newport.
1:00 p.m.	Lunch.
2:30 p.m.	See the aquarium.
3:30 p.m.	Continue up the coast to Astoria.
6:30 p.m.	Cross the Columbia into Washington. Camp at Fort Canby State Park.

Travel Route: Florence to Astoria (182 miles)
Follow US 101 north all the way to the Washington state line, a distance of 186 miles. The first part of the trip, between Florence and Newport, contains the coast's most-photographed lighthouses and rocky seascapes as well as easily accessible tide pools. The area around Lincoln City, within easy reach of Portland, has the most commercial development. North of there the towns are older, quainter, and less prosperous.

After visiting Astoria, unless you plan to spend tonight there, cross the mouth of the Columbia River on the high arch of the 4-mile-long Astoria Bridge ($1.50 toll), and you're back in Washington. Completed in 1966, this bridge was the last link in US 101 up the entire Pacific coast from Mexico to Canada. Ten miles farther up the highway, take Highway 103 west (left) to Ilwaco and follow the signs to Fort Canby State Park.

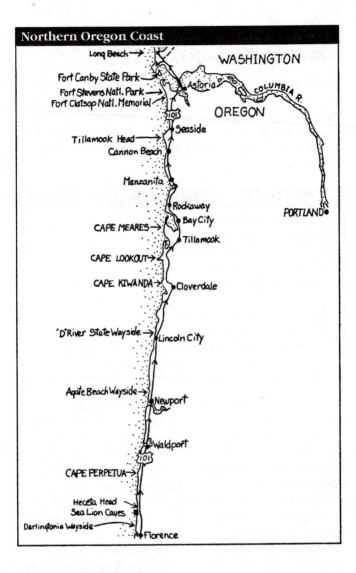

Northern Oregon Coast

Sightseeing Highlights

Florence—Adjoined by Oregon Dunes National Recreation Area to the south and Siuslaw National Forest to the north, within an hour's drive of more than half of Oregon's coastal parks, this is the premier resort town of the central coast. Like Bandon, Florence has a recently gentrified waterfront Old Town. The main local holiday is the Rhododendron Festival, held annually for more than eighty years on the third weekend of May. Besides the usual small-town events, such as a parade, carnival, queen coronation, pancake breakfast, and soap box derby—and, of course, a rhododendron show—the festival features the Sunday afternoon Silver Trails Slug Race. (If you don't own a slug, you can rent one of these slimy little critters from local entrepreneurs.)

▲**Darlingtonia Botanical Wayside**—If you find bizarre flora intriguing, stroll the half-mile nature trail 6 miles north of Florence for a close-up look at carnivorous cobra lilies. Don't worry—they only eat insects.

▲▲**Sea Lion Caves**—The Oregon coast's most famous commercial tourist attraction is 12 miles north of Florence. When the weather is lousy, the sea lions huddle inside the large cave, the only known year-round sea lion rookery on the U.S. mainland. The $6 elevator ride ($3.50 for children ages 6 to 15) down to the cave is well worth the price. On warm sunny days, the sea lions bask on rocky islands outside, and you can save the admission fee by watching them through binoculars from the overlook just around the next curve in the highway.

▲▲**Heceta Head Lighthouse**—A short distance north of the Sea Lion Caves, this is probably the most-photographed lighthouse on the Pacific coast. You may experience a sense of déjà vu as you pause at the overlook to snap your own shot of it.

▲▲▲**Cape Perpetua**—This is my favorite spot on the Oregon coast. Captain James Cook, the British explorer who later was the first white man to discover both New Zealand and the Hawaiian Islands, apparently didn't share my opinion. While searching for the Northwest Passage and naming practically every point of land along the coast for one saint or another, Cook designated this headland for St. Perpetua, an obscure third-century Carthaginian, after a March storm had held his ship here—"perpetually," it seemed—until he and his crew grew sick of the sight of it. From the visitor center, 12 miles north of the Sea Lion Caves, a short hike across lava flows takes you down to a wonderful series of tide pools where you may discover sea anemones, starfish, sea urchins, hermit crabs, mussels, barnacles, limpets, and whelks. Look, touch, but please don't remove (or eat) them. On the way, you'll see a shell mound, the only remaining trace of Indian habitation along the coast. Very little is known about these Indians—except that over the centuries they ate a lot of clams. Some of these piles of discarded shells are more than 40 feet high. Other trails from the visitor center go uphill through old-growth forest with giant spruce trees. The longest, 4½-mile Cook's Ridge Trail, takes you to the top of the 800-foot headland for magnificent views of the coast. During whale-watching season, mid-December through May, wait patiently in the visitor center hoping to glimpse a cetacean through the high-powered telescope.

▲▲**Mark O. Hatfield Marine Science Center**—In the town of Newport, exit US 101 just before the art deco Yaquina Bay Bridge. This University of Oregon oceanographic research facility houses a free public aquarium, open 10:00 a.m. to 4:00 p.m., May through September until 6:00 p.m., where exhibits include more than a dozen large tanks containing native fish and other Oregon coast sea life, including many varieties of brightly colored anemones and sea pens, as well as a huge octopus. Another display, showing how beach trash cripples and kills sea creatures, is gruesome enough to haunt you whenever you start to toss aside a pop-top or plastic six-pack holder.

▲**Agate Beach Wayside**—About 2½ miles north of Newport, this is a promising spot to beachcomb for semi-precious beach pebbles. The Newport Chamber of Commerce distributes a pamphlet, *Agates: Their Formation and How to Hunt for Them.*

The "D" River—Short name. Short river. World's shortest, they claim. Flows 440 feet from Devil's Lake to the ocean. Lincoln City's major tourist attraction. If it weren't advertised, you'd never notice it.

Lincoln City—Strategically located where the main route from Portland joins the coast highway, Lincoln City is the Oregon coast's boomtown. This "city" was formerly five separate towns, collectively known as the "Twenty Miracle Miles." Though it has a year-round population of only 6,000, driving through it on US 101 seems to take forever. To find the town's namesake, turn left one block past the turnoff to Devil's Lake State Park and look for Lincoln on the Prairie, a 14-foot bronze sculpture depicting Honest Abe as a young lawyer, on horseback, reading a book. Maybe it's a guidebook; he's a long way from home.

▲**Northern Oregon Coast**—After you leave Lincoln City, US 101 narrows and winds as you wonder what happened to all the traffic. Resort development seems to have bypassed the stretch of coast highway from here north almost to Seaside. Along this, the low-rent district of the Oregon coast, quiet little towns that could stand a fresh coat of paint suggest what life on the rest of the Oregon coast must have been like forty years ago.

If you have time to spare, turn left where the highway veers inland, about 15 miles north of Lincoln City, for a 34-mile detour with surprisingly diverse scenery. Follow the coastline road through Pacific City, past Cape Kiwanda and Cape Lookout state parks (two more world-class seascape views), through the village of Oceanside, which looks out on Three Arches National Wildlife Refuge, one of North America's largest seabird nesting grounds in the spring and year-round home to a large sea lion colony, to Cape Meares, where you'll find an abandoned lighthouse and a giant, ancient Sitka spruce known as the Octopus Tree. This relaxed drive, which takes about half an hour longer than the main highway, not counting stops, brings you back to US 101 at Tillamook, a dairy farming town that bills itself as "The Cheese Capital of Oregon." Stop to sample the local products at the Blue Heron French Cheese Factory. You can tour the Tillamook Cheese Factory, about a mile farther up the road, where you'll also find freshly made ice cream.

▲▲**Cannon Beach**—Another 40 miles along the coast on US 101 will bring you to this artists' colony. Take time to browse in the art and craft galleries. The local landmark, just offshore, is Haystack Rock. Around the base of the rock, tide pools contain a particularly colorful assortment of sea life. The year's biggest local event is Sandcastle Day, the third Saturday in June, which draws 1,000 contestants and up to 35,000 spectators each year. This sand sculpture competition has achieved such renown that the local chamber of commerce has been asked to help organize similar contests in North Carolina, California, and Australia.

▲**Seaside**—The oldest resort town on the Oregon coast, Seaside has been a tourist mecca since the 1870s. Even earlier, this site was the end of Lewis and Clark's trek to the Pacific, as a reconstruction of the salt cairn where members of their party boiled seawater into salt attests. It's near the south end of the promenade. Recent big resort and convention developments have obscured some of Seaside's old-fashioned tourist town quaintness, and the decades-old Fun Zone amusement park seems in danger of being overwhelmed by video games. In midsummer, however, the high-energy crush of fun seekers on the 2-mile beachfront promenade is as exciting as ever.

▲**Beach Drive**—At low tide you can drive your car or camper along the hard-surface beach for 10 miles from Gearhart to Fort Stevens State Park. The Beach Drive begins at Marion and Tenth Street in Gearhart, just north of Seaside.

▲**Fort Stevens State Park**—Take a short detour north from US 101 at Skipanon, around the peninsula that shelters Astoria, to see what's left of military fortifications built during the Civil War to protect the Columbia River. As it turned out, the South never invaded Oregon, but in World War II Fort Stevens was fired on by a Japanese submarine. The most interesting sight here is the 1906 wreckage of the 287-foot British schooner *Peter Iredale* on the beach.

▲▲**Fort Clatsop National Memorial**—On the way to Fort Stevens, this is a reconstruction of Lewis and Clark's end-of-the-trail fortress, where their party shivered and grumbled through the gloomy, stormy winter of 1805. "Winds violent Trees falling in every derection, whorl winds, with gusts of Hail & Thunder," wrote Clark (never much of a speller). "Oh how disagreeable our Situation

dureing this dreadful winter." The visitor center has audiovisual and museum exhibits on the expedition, and
rangers in frontier costume demonstrate pioneer skills during the summer months. Open 8:00 a.m. to 6:00 p.m. mid-
June through Labor Day, until 5:00 p.m. the rest of the
year; admission $2 per adult, free for children 12 and
under and seniors 61 and up.

▲▲**Astoria**—In 1811, fur trader John Astor founded the
first permanent settlement in the Pacific Northwest here. A
replica of his small blockhouse fort is at 15th and
Exchange streets. The premier attraction in town, however,
is the 123-foot Astoria Column atop Coxcomb Hill. Climb
the stairway to the observation deck for an incomparable
view of the town and the river mouth.

Murals on the column depict the city's history. To get
there, drive—or, better yet, walk—along Eighth Street
and turn left up Franklin Avenue, lined with nineteenth-
century mansions; return down Grand Avenue, paralleling
Franklin one block uphill, with equally magnificent historic homes. For a look inside one of these residences,
stop at the Captain Flavel House at 441 Eighth Street. The
high point among the museum exhibits is its collection of
photographs showing the wreckage of ships that didn't
quite make the treacherous passage from the ocean
around the sandbars at the mouth of the river. The museum
is open from 10:00 a.m. to 5:00 p.m. daily, May through
October, and 11:00 a.m. to 4:00 p.m. the rest of the year.
Admission is $4 for adults, $2 for senior citizens, $2 for
children ages 6 to 12. The admission charge also covers
the Heritage Center Museum in the restored former city
hall at 1618 Exchange Street, open the same hours as the
Flavel House. Nearby, at 1793 Marine Drive, the Columbia
River Maritime Museum is the best museum of its kind in
the Pacific Northwest. See the Columbia lightship (an old
seagoing lighthouse that guided ships into the mouth of
the Columbia) anchored beside the museum. The ship
and maritime museum are open from 9:30 a.m. to 5:00
p.m. daily; admission is $5 for adults, $4 for senior citizens, $2 for children ages 6 to 18.

Camping

Fort Stevens State Park has Oregon's largest campground—605 sites, many with full hookups. Reservations are required from Memorial Day weekend through Labor Day weekend. The reservation procedure is the same as that for Honeyman State Park, described in Day 18. The address is: Fort Stevens, Hammond, OR 97121.

What's that? You're not sure you want to stay in Oregon's largest campground? Well, okay . . . drive across the river and over to the southern end of Long Beach Peninsula, where you'll find **Fort Canby State Park**. This park is the site of another Civil War era fort and another Lewis and Clark "end of the trail." (Clark described in his journal standing where Cape Disappointment Lighthouse is now and "beholding with estonishment this emence Ocian.") There are a total of 250 campsites in several campgrounds scattered through the 1,700-acre park. Fort Canby State Park also operates on a reservation system during the summer months. The reservation system is the same as that described in Day 6 for Moran State Park. The address is: Fort Canby State Park, Box 488, Ilwaco, WA 98642. The park also has a Lewis and Clark Interpretive Center, hiking trails, and beaches. For beachcombers, Waikiki Beach (which bears no resemblance to its Hawaiian namesake) has impressive piles of driftwood.

Lodging

One of Astoria's grand Victorian mansions rents rooms. It's the **Franklin St. Station B&B Inn** at 1140 Franklin Street, Astoria, OR 97103, (503) 325-4314. There are only four guest rooms and suites, in the $60 range, so make reservations well in advance. Astoria also has less extraordinary, but perfectly acceptable, accommodations, such as the **Red Lion Inn**, 400 Industry Street, at the junction of US 101 and US 30, (503) 325-7373, with a view of the marina and river. Rates are $83 to $88 in the summer, $70 to $79 off-season. The **Crest Motel**, 533 Leif Erickson Drive, east of town on Highway 30, (503) 325-3141, also overlooks the Columbia River. Rates for a double room start around $46.

Food

Stock up on picnic supplies in downtown Cannon Beach at **Osburn's "World Famous" Grocery Store and Delicatessen**, a "thrifty gourmet" grocery store in one of the town's oldest buildings. Cannon Beach also has numerous small specialty food shops that sell seafood, baked goods, candy, and wine. If **Maxine's Produce** is selling strawberry shortcake at its stand just south of Astoria, buy some. It's the biggest shortcake bargain I've ever seen, and the berries are fresh.

The **Ships Inn** in Astoria is the best fish 'n' chips place I've found in the Northwest. All the locals go there. Try it and find out why.

OLYMPIC COAST TO HOH RAIN FOREST

Today's drive starts out as a nightmarish trip through the industrial heartland of the nation's timber industry, but ends sublimely in Olympic National Park's Hoh Rain Forest. In this temperate-zone jungle, one of only a few in the world, giant trees drip moss and sprout licorice ferns. The forest floor is so thick with vegetation that you won't even hear your own footsteps in the primeval stillness.

Suggested Schedule

8:00 a.m.	Drive to Queets.
12:00 noon	Visit Olympic National Park beach, picnic.
1:30 p.m.	Drive to Hoh Rain Forest.
3:00 p.m.	Explore Hoh Rain Forest. Camp there.

Travel Route: Fort Canby to Hoh Rain Forest (161 miles)

From Ilwaco, stay on US 101 for 116 miles to reach Kalaloch Lodge at the southern end of the Olympic National Park coastal unit. Twenty-six more miles on US 101 will bring you to the turnoff on your right for the 19-mile drive to Hoh Rain Forest.

Unlike in Oregon, most of US 101 in Washington is well inland from the coast. The first leg of the drive takes you through attractive wetland marshes, astonishing in their abundance of bird life. As you reach the evergreen forests, you'll find yourself in the middle of one of the major battle zones of the Spotted Owl Wars.

You'll dodge monster log trucks along this stretch of 101. You'll view clear-cut devastation that looks a lot like Mount St. Helens's ash-blasted slopes. And you'll see towns where signs on all the houses and stores shout that they depend on timber dollars—angry outcries from people who believe their way of life is being sacrificed for the sake of a small, nocturnal bird.

In these parts, it is better not to sport an environmentalist slogan on your car bumper or T-shirt. Local sentiments run very high. Timber-dependent families truly believe that *they* are the real environmentalists and the Sierra Club, National Audubon Society et al. are dangerous "preservationist" extremists.

You'll pass through Aberdeen, the largest lumber shipping port in the United States. An hour's drive to the north through sterile new-growth industrial forests, you'll cross the Quinault Indian Reservation, clear-cut bare by non-Indians. Finally, just outside the Hoh Rain Forest national park boundary, you'll see former rain forest that was destroyed decades ago and still shows no signs of ever growing back. As you enter the virgin rain forest, the small remaining parcel of our nation's most magnificent woodland, the tragedy hits home like a hammer between the eyes: our endangered ancient forest is *not* a "renewable resource."

Nor, for that matter, are the families that have made their homes in this beautiful region and their livelihoods in logging for generations. Is there a solution to the crisis in the Pacific Northwest's forest products industry? It would be nice, in some future edition of *2 to 22 Days in the Pacific Northwest*, to look back on the Spotted Owl Wars as a quaint and slightly silly crisis of bygone days, sort of like San Juan Island's Pig War. Some locals believe the Olympic Peninsula's burgeoning tourist industry will supplement the declining timber business. Others damn well don't think so. We'll see.

Sightseeing Highlights
Quinault Indian Reservation—From Lake Quinault to the coast, US 101 follows the northern boundary of the largest Indian reservation on the Olympic Peninsula. Most of the tribe's 1,000 people live far from the highway, near the river, where travel is prohibited unless you have tribal permission, which is difficult to obtain. The Quinaults make their living fishing for salmon and processing it in the tribal cannery, thanks to a landmark court decision that restored their fishing rights under a treaty that had

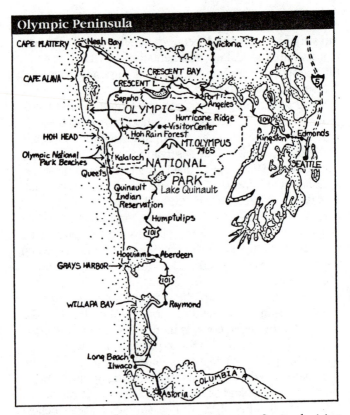

Olympic Peninsula

long been ignored. The tribe is also known for its decision to ban non-Indians from a once-popular beach in the coastal town of Queets. White men, they said, leave too much trash. The chief of this small tribe spends much of his time in Washington, D.C., where he is the nation's foremost lobbyist for Native American rights.

▲**Quinault and Queets rain forests**—North of the Quinault reservation, two roads run east from the main highway to trailheads in a remote corner of Olympic National Park. They provide access to two other pockets of temperate rain forest much like the Hoh Rain Forest (see below). The difference is, these two less-known areas do not have national park visitor centers, rangers on duty, admission booths at the entrance, or hordes of visitors. The Quinault Rain Forest can be reached from the road on either the north or south shore of Lake Quinault, just east of the main highway. The roads pass through a lakeside summer homes area and then continue as an unpaved road to a campground and a forest trailhead into the national park wilderness area. The Queets Rain Forest, reached by a shorter side road about 20 miles farther north on US 101, has a 3-mile nature trail through the forest as well as a longer trail that leads along the Queets River deep into the national park.

▲▲**Olympic National Park: Coast Unit**—Beginning 2 miles north of Queets, the seashore wilderness strip of Olympic National Park extends for 57 miles to the north, interrupted only by three very small coastal Indian reservations, Hoh, Quillayute, and Ozette. Only the south 14 miles are accessible by road, along the stretch of US 101 known as the Kalaloch-Ruby Beach Highway. For most of the drive, you can't see the ocean or beach from the highway. Stop at any (or all) of seven pullouts, where short trails lead down to the beach. This coastline feels wild and untouched; wander it and dream. Watch for tracks of raccoons, otters, and even bears in the wet sand. If the lure of this coastline captures your imagination, and the weather is fair, you can walk for many miles north of Ruby Beach and the Hoh reservation without seeing another human being. Before undertaking a long hike, stop at the little National Park Service information station across the highway near Kalaloch (pronounced "CLAY-lock") Lodge and pick up the *Strip of Wilderness* brochure that tells you how to circumvent treacherous headlands on overland trails.

(Note: You could spend the rest of today on the coast, perhaps staying at Kalaloch Lodge or the nearby campground, visit the Hoh Rain Forest tomorrow morning, and still have time tomorrow and the next day to see the Sightseeing Highlights described in Days 21 and 22.)

▲▲▲**Olympic National Park, Hoh Rain Forest**—About 12 miles past where US 101 leaves the coast unit of the national park, watch for the road that exits on your right (east) to the Hoh Rain Forest. The road into the rain forest is 19 miles long.

You've already seen a wide variety of forests on this tour—ancient forests, second-growth forests, industrial fir forests, dry-side pine forests, California redwood forests—but you'll never find another one like the Hoh Rain Forest. This and similar areas in the Quinault and Queets river valleys not far to the south make up one of only three temperate-zone rain forests in the world. (The others are in New Zealand and southern Chile.) The Hoh Valley receives an average of 145 inches of rain a year—more than four times as much as Seattle. As a result, every square inch of ground is covered with vegetation. Ferns and sorrel form such a thick carpet on the forest floor that tree seedlings have a hard time taking root, so trees grow in neat rows from older trees that have fallen and decayed. Moss drips from branches, and licorice ferns grow from the sides of living trees without ever touching the earth. Sitka spruce reach 300 feet in height and 23 feet in diameter (considerably larger than they grow in Sitka, Alaska, for which they are named, and about the same height as California's giant redwoods). Black-tailed deer wander the forest without fear, and Roosevelt elk descend from the mountains to graze here in autumn. Colorful harlequin ducks are also a common sight. Admission, which covers all units of Olympic National Park for 7 days, is $3 per vehicle May through September, free at other times of year.

After a stop at the visitor center, walk the 1-mile Hall of Mosses Trail. It's beautiful but too short. For more, take the 1.3-mile Spruce Nature Trail. These are the only two short trails in the rain forest. If they're not enough to satisfy your fascination with this damp verdant wonderland, you have two options: (1) hike them again, or (2) hike part of the Hoh River Trail. This 17-mile trail goes up to the base of the glaciers on Mount Olympus and is the shortest route for mountaineers climbing Olympic National Park's highest mountain (7,965 feet). You don't have to walk all the way. The first 12½ miles are through rain forest; go as far as you like. You must first obtain a free wilderness permit at the visitor center.

Camping

The Hoh Rain Forest has a 95-site national park campground with a dumping station but no hookups. The fee is $6. There is also a larger national park campground, with comparable facilities and rates, near the ocean at Kalaloch.

Lodging

There is no lodging at the Hoh Rain Forest. The best plan for visitors to the west side of Olympic National Park who do not wish to camp is to stay at **Kalaloch Lodge** overlooking the ocean, on US 101, 26 miles south of the turnoff to the Hoh Rain Forest. Check in first, then drive to the rain forest for the afternoon, and return to the lodge for dinner. Rooms start around $125 in season (June through October) and on weekends year-round, $55 off-season. Private cabins cost more. For reservations, contact Kalaloch Lodge, H.S. 80, Box 1100, Forks, WA 98331, or call (206) 962-2271.

Lower-priced lodging as well as some newly built resort facilities and several restaurants can be found at Forks, on US 101, 14 miles north of the turnoff to the Hoh Rain Forest. The **Forks Motel** on US 101, (206) 374-6243, has large guest units starting at $42 a night. The **Manitou Lodge** offers peaceful bed and breakfast accommodations at $55 per night double. Call (206) 374-6295. Reservations are essential if you plan to visit the west coast of the Olympic Peninsula during the summer months, since the fledgling lodging industry has not caught up with the rapid growth of tourism in the area.

NEAH BAY

Today's highlight is the greatest archaeological discovery ever made in the Pacific Northwest, a collection of artifacts from a 500-year-old coastal Indian village, lovingly preserved and displayed by the people whose ancestors made them.

Suggested Schedule

9:00 a.m.	Leave Hoh Rain Forest.
11:00 a.m.	Arrive in Neah Bay. Visit the Makah Museum.
1:00 p.m.	Drive to Cape Flattery.
1:30 p.m.	Picnic at Cape Flattery.
3:00 p.m.	Return to US 101 and drive to Lake Crescent.
4:30 p.m.	Camp at Lake Crescent or stay at the lodge there.

Travel Route: Hoh Rain Forest to Neah Bay (61 miles) and Neah Bay to Lake Crescent (50 miles)

Return to US 101, turn right, and drive north for 25 miles to the little town of Sappho. Turn left on the road marked to Neah Bay. Ten more miles will bring you to the intersection with State Highway 112. Turn left (west), and in 6 miles you'll reach the northern coastline of the Olympic Peninsula at Clallam Bay. It's 20 more slow miles along the narrow, winding road, always in sight of the seashore with views 15 miles across the Strait of Juan de Fuca to Vancouver Island in Canada. As you enter the poor but honest Indian fishing village of Neah Bay on the Makah Indian Reservation, watch for the Neah Bay Cultural and Research Center on your left.

From Neah Bay, retrace your route to Sappho and rejoin US 101 eastbound (left). From Sappho, it's 17 miles to the western tip of Lake Crescent.

Sightseeing Highlights
▲▲▲Makah Museum, Neah Bay Cultural and Research Center—This is the most unusual and rewarding Native American museum in the Pacific Northwest. It houses the artifacts excavated from the 500-year-old village at Ozette, 15 miles south along the Pacific coast. (Excavations at the Ozette site have been completed, and the site has been reburied to protect any remaining artifacts for future generations of archaeologists. There's little to attract visitors—except for one of the peninsula's largest lakes and a 3-mile hike to the wilderness coastline at the northern end of Olympic National Park's coastal unit.)

While dampness has rotted and destroyed most Northwest Coast Indian artifacts, the village of Ozette was buried in a mudslide and preserved in perfect condition for five centuries, until its discovery in 1970. Beautifully displayed under tribal supervision at the Makah Museum, the items unearthed at Ozette evoke a vivid picture of these people who harpooned whales from canoes, cultivated potatoes that somehow got here from Peru, and made tools of metal fragments washed ashore from the wreckage of Asian sailing vessels. A profound sense of mystery surrounds these articles of everyday life from a forgotten time. When you've viewed all the exhibits, sit and meditate for a while inside the longhouse replica, where recorded voices murmur softly in the Makah language, and let the magic carry you back through centuries. Although the Makah people clung to their traditional way of life until the beginning of the twentieth century, their descendants today don't remember much more about it than you'll know after visiting this fascinating one-of-a-kind museum. The gift shop carries Native American arts and crafts as well as books on Indian subjects.

The museum is open daily from 10:00 a.m. to 5:00 p.m., closed Mondays and Tuesdays from mid-September through May. Admission is $4 for adults, $3 for full-time students and senior citizens, free for children under age 4.

▲Cape Flattery—Beyond Neah Bay, the only paved road ends at an Air Force Station. From there, a dirt road leads northwest for about 5 miles to the Cape Flattery Trailhead. A short (half-mile, half-hour each way) trail through the woods takes you to Cape Flattery, where you can stand on the northwesternmost point in the lower 48 United States.

For a longer hike, take the dirt road that goes south from the Air Force Station across the Waatch River bridge. It goes 7 miles, past Hobuck and Sooes beaches, to the Shi-Shi Beach Trailhead. A 3-mile hike (allow 90 minutes each way) will bring you to Shi-Shi Beach, a wild and virtually untouched beach where yours will be the only footprints. There are tide pools and huge rocks that lean at improbable angles. Nearby, old shipwrecks lie offshore.

▲**Soleduck Falls**—At the end of the Soleduck road off US 101, a short distance past Sol Duc Hot Springs (an old spa resort where there is a campground and privately owned hot springs pools), a lovely 1-mile trail runs from the trailhead to a powerful waterfall that crashes through a small gorge. Along the road are several other short trails, including the Salmon Cascades Trail and the Ancient Groves Nature Trail. A network of long trails begins near Soleduck Falls and penetrates to the heart of the national park wilderness. One of the trails goes for 17 miles, over a mile-high mountain pass, before joining the trail from the Hoh Rain Forest to the summit of Mount Olympus.

▲**Lake Crescent**—Eight-and-a-half miles long and over 600 feet deep, this lake on the northern boundary of Olympic National Park is the largest in the park. From the Storm King Ranger Station beside US 101 near the midpoint of the lake, a mile-long trail takes you up to 90-foot Marymere Falls. The last part of the trail is quite steep.

Camping

The largest of several national park campgrounds near Lake Crescent is **Fairholm Campground** on North Shore Road by the lake, with 87 sites. Others nearby are **Altaire Campground** (29 sites) and **Elwha Campground** (41 sites), both a few miles south on Elwha River Road, which turns off US 101 17 miles beyond the lake, 9 miles west of Port Angeles, and **Soleduck Campground** (84 sites), 12

miles south on the Soleduck Road, which turns off US 101
a short distance west of the lake.

Lodging and Food

At **Lake Crescent Lodge** on the lakeshore, rooms and
cottages range from $68 to $121 a night. The lodge has a
dining room and a cocktail lounge. It is open May through
October only. For reservations, contact National Park
Concessions, Inc., H.C. 62, Box 11, Port Angeles, WA
98362, or call (206) 928-3211.

Nearby, 3 miles off US 101 via East Beach Road on the
northeast end of the lake, is **Log Cabin Resort**, with
motel units, cabins, an RV park, a restaurant, and a grocery store. Rates start at $50 a night. For reservations, con-
tact them at 6540 East Beach Road, Port Angeles, WA
98362, or call (206) 928-3325.

If Lake Crescent Lodge and Log Cabin Resort are full—
as they usually are in the summer months unless you
made reservations far in advance—you'll find plenty of
motels in nearby Port Angeles, as well as a number of
good bed and breakfasts. Try **Bayton's On-the-Bluff**,
824 West 4th Street, (206) 457-5569, from $65 per night;
Bavarian Inn, 1126 East 7th Street, (206) 457-4098 (call
after 2:30 p.m.), from $80 per night; or **Bed and Break-
fast at Our House**, 218 Whidbey Avenue, (206) 452-6338,
$65 per night. A favorite Port Angeles restaurant is the
Café Garden, 1506 East 1st Street, 457-4611, where
specialties include Dungeness crab cakes and excellent
stir-fries.

If you wish to spend the night at Neah Bay, your best
motel bets are **Thunderbird Resort**, (206) 645-2450, and
Tyee Motel & RV Park, (206) 645-2223.

HURRICANE RIDGE AND RETURN TO SEATTLE

A walk through the alpine meadows of Hurricane Ridge, high in the mountains of Olympic National Park, is the climax of your Northwest tour. Tonight you'll be back in Seattle.

Suggested Schedule

8:30 a.m.	Leave Lake Crescent.
9:30 a.m.	Drive up Hurricane Ridge.
10:30 a.m.	Hike and explore on Hurricane Ridge. Bring a picnic lunch.
2:30 p.m. (or later)	Drive back down Hurricane Ridge Highway to the National Park Visitor Center.
3:30 p.m.	See the visitor center.
4:00 p.m.	Leave Port Angeles and drive to Kingston.
5:50 or 6:30 p.m	Kingston Ferry to Edmonds.
7:00 p.m.	Welcome back to Seattle!

Travel Route: Lake Crescent to Kingston (113 miles)
At the eastern tip of Lake Crescent, take the road that turns off along the lake's north shore, goes through the village of Piedmont, then crosses Highway 112 and loops around past Crescent Bay, rejoining Highway 112 in a few miles. Where the highway merges with US 101, turn right (southwest) and drive about 2 miles to the "Heart O' The Hills" road. (This Crescent Bay detour meanders off the beaten path; you can skip it and save about half an hour by driving directly east on US 101 from Lake Crescent to the "Heart O' The Hills" road, just past Elwha.)

After about 6 miles, the road joins the Hurricane Ridge Highway. Follow it up to Hurricane Ridge.

Descending from Hurricane Ridge, stay on the main road, which will take you into downtown Port Angeles.

From Port Angeles, follow US 101 east for 38 miles to the Highway 104 turnoff, 3 miles south of Discovery Bay. Follow Highway 104 for 24 miles, and you'll find yourself at the Kingston ferry dock.

Sightseeing Highlights

▲**Crescent Bay**—In the 1890s, the logging town of Port Crescent, just north of what is now Tongue Point County Park, was one of the largest communities on the peninsula's Juan de Fuca coast. All that's left is the graveyard. Few people come this way any more, and the beach is never crowded.

▲▲▲**Olympic National Park: Hurricane Ridge**—The park's ultimate scenic drive is open (and well traveled) year-round. In the winter and early spring, Hurricane Ridge is a popular snow-play area, with cross country skis, sleds, and snowshoes for rent at the lodge. Snow reaches a depth of 20 feet and lingers through June. In the summer, the ridge is a wonderland of subalpine meadows, where the wildflowers include several subspecies found nowhere else on earth, such as Plett's violet, Piper's bellflower, and the Olympic Mountain daisy. Unique wildlife, too, has evolved in these mountains: the Olympic marmot, Olympic chipmunk, and Olympic snow mole.

The views from 5,200-foot Hurricane Ridge defy comparison with any others in the Pacific Northwest. To the north you can see Port Angeles, the Strait of Juan de Fuca, the San Juan Islands, and the Canadian coast—all a mile below you. To the south you can see the immensity of the national park's wilderness interior, more than 600,000 acres of rugged mountain peaks, all inaccessible by road. For the best view, drive the 8-mile Alpine Drive along the ridgeline to Obstruction Point.

The interior of Olympic National Park contains over 600 miles of hiking trails. For breathtaking hiking, leave the crowds behind and follow the trail that goes from Obstruction Point east for 2 miles to Elk Mountain. It continues for another 6 miles one way to Deer Park.

Another trail from Obstruction Point follows the ridgeline to the south and then descends steeply to Grand Lake and Moose Lake, a distance of 3 miles each way. Allow all day for this one. Shorter walking trails are found all along the Alpine Drive.

On the return trip from Hurricane Ridge, stop at Olympic National Park's main visitor center, the Port Angeles Visitor Center and Pioneer Memorial Museum, where the road enters the outskirts of Port Angeles (3002 Mount Angeles Road). Even though you've already seen the park from several angles in the past three days, it is so vast and complex and changes so much with the weather and the seasons, that the exhibits and audiovisual programs here can add a new dimension of understanding to what you've experienced. Displays feature flora and fauna, geology, history, and Indian culture. The visitor center is open daily from 8:00 a.m. to 6:30 p.m. July through Labor Day, 8:00 a.m. to 4:00 p.m. the rest of the year. Admission is free.

▲**Dungeness Spit**—Famed for the Dungeness crabs harvested here, which are a popular gourmet seafood dish around Puget Sound, this 7-mile-long natural sand hook is a national wildlife refuge, a nesting area for waterfowl and a stopover in the fall and winter for huge flocks of ducks and snow geese. Pay $2 at the entrance in adjoining Dungeness Spit State Park and walk along the sandy beach—with the waters of the Strait of Juan de Fuca on both sides—as far as you want. If you hike the full length of the spit, which few visitors do, you will come to an 1857 lighthouse that is open for touring.

Return to Seattle on the Kingston Ferry

The ferry leaves the Kingston dock approximately every hour until 11:10 p.m., costs $6.65, takes 30 minutes to cross Puget Sound, and lets you off in Edmonds. Then follow the main street south from the ferry dock: it will return you to Interstate 5, 11 miles north of downtown Seattle, where this northwestern journey began three weeks ago. I hope you've enjoyed using this book as much as I've enjoyed writing it.

INDEX

Other Books from John Muir Publications

Travel Books by Rick Steves
**Asia Through the Back Door,
4th ed.,** 400 pp. $16.95
**Europe 101: History, Art, and
Culture for the Traveler,
4th ed.,** 372 pp. $15.95
**Mona Winks: Self-Guided
Tours of Europe's Top
Museums, 2nd ed.,** 456 pp.
$16.95
**Rick Steves' Best of the
Baltics and Russia, 1995
ed.** 144 pp. $9.95
**Rick Steves' Best of Europe,
1995 ed.,** 544 pp. $16.95
**Rick Steves' Best of France,
Belgium, and the
Netherlands, 1995 ed.,** 240
pp. $12.95
**Rick Steves' Best of
Germany, Austria, and
Switzerland, 1995 ed.,** 240
pp. $12.95
**Rick Steves' Best of Great
Britain, 1995 ed.,** 192 pp.
$11.95
**Rick Steves' Best of Italy,
1995 ed.,** 208 pp. $11.95
**Rick Steves' Best of
Scandinavia, 1995 ed.,** 192
pp. $11.95
**Rick Steves' Best of Spain
and Portugal, 1995 ed.,** 192
pp. $11.95
**Rick Steves' Europe Through
the Back Door, 13th ed.,**
480 pp. $17.95
**Rick Steves' French Phrase
Book, 2nd ed.,** 112 pp. $4.95
**Rick Steves' German Phrase
Book, 2nd ed.,** 112 pp. $4.95
**Rick Steves' Italian Phrase
Book, 2nd ed.,** 112 pp. $4.95
**Rick Steves' Spanish and
Portuguese Phrase Book,
2nd ed.,** 288 pp. $5.95
**Rick Steves'
French/German/Italian
Phrase Book,** 288 pp. $6.95

A Natural Destination Series
**Belize: A Natural Destination,
2nd ed.,** 304 pp. $16.95

**Costa Rica: A Natural
Destination, 3rd ed.,** 400
pp. $17.95
**Guatemala: A Natural
Destination,** 336 pp. $16.95

Undiscovered Islands Series
**Undiscovered Islands of the
Caribbean, 3rd ed.,** 264 pp.
$14.95
**Undiscovered Islands of the
Mediterranean, 2nd ed.,** 256
pp. $13.95
**Undiscovered Islands of the
U.S. and Canadian West
Coast,** 288 pp. $12.95

For Birding Enthusiasts
**The Birder's Guide to Bed
and Breakfasts: U.S.
and Canada,** 288 pp.
$15.95
**The Visitor's Guide to the
Birds of the Central
National Parks: U.S. and
Canada,** 400 pp. $15.95
**The Visitor's Guide to the
Birds of the Eastern
National Parks: U.S. and
Canada,** 400 pp. $15.95
**The Visitor's Guide to the
Birds of the Rocky
Mountain National Parks:
U.S. and Canada,** 432 pp.
$15.95

Unique Travel Series
Each is 112 pages and $10.95
paperback.
Unique Arizona
Unique California
Unique Colorado
Unique Florida
Unique New England
Unique New Mexico
Unique Texas
Unique Washington

**2 to 22 Days Itinerary
Planners**
**2 to 22 Days in the American
Southwest, 1995 ed.,** 192
pp. $11.95

2 to 22 Days in Asia, 192 pp. $10.95

2 to 22 Days in Australia, 192 pp. $10.95

2 to 22 Days in California, 1995 ed., 192 pp. $11.95

2 to 22 Days in Eastern Canada, 1995 ed., 240 pp. $12.95

2 to 22 Days in Florida, 1995 ed., 192 pp. $11.95

2 to 22 Days Around the Great Lakes, 1995 ed., 192 pp. $11.95

2 to 22 Days in Hawaii, 1995 ed., 192 pp. $11.95

2 to 22 Days in New England, 1995 ed., 192 pp. $11.95

2 to 22 Days in New Zealand, 192 pp. $10.95

2 to 22 Days in the Pacific Northwest, 1995 ed., 192 pp. $11.95

2 to 22 Days in the Rockies, 1995 ed., 192 pp. $11.95

2 to 22 Days in Texas, 1995 ed., 192 pp. $11.95

2 to 22 Days in Thailand, 192 pp. $10.95

22 Days Around the World, 264 pp. $13.95

Other Terrific Travel Titles

The 100 Best Small Art Towns in America, 224 pp. $12.95

Elderhostels: The Students' Choice, 2nd ed., 304 pp. $15.95

Environmental Vacations: Volunteer Projects to Save the Planet, 2nd ed., 248 pp. $16.95

A Foreign Visitor's Guide to America, 224 pp. $12.95

Great Cities of Eastern Europe, 256 pp. $16.95

Indian America: A Traveler's Companion, 3rd ed., 432 pp. $18.95

Interior Furnishings Southwest, 256 pp. $19.95

Opera! The Guide to Western Europe's Great Houses, 296 pp. $18.95

Paintbrushes and Pistols:

How the Taos Artists Sold the West, 288 pp. $17.95

The People's Guide to Mexico, 9th ed., 608 pp. $18.95

Ranch Vacations: The Complete Guide to Guest and Resort, Fly-Fishing, and Cross-Country Skiing Ranches, 3rd ed., 512 pp. $19.95

The Shopper's Guide to Art and Crafts in the Hawaiian Islands, 272 pp. $13.95

The Shopper's Guide to Mexico, 224 pp. $9.95

Understanding Europeans, 272 pp. $14.95

A Viewer's Guide to Art: A Glossary of Gods, People, and Creatures, 144 pp. $10.95

Watch It Made in the U.S.A.: A Visitor's Guide to the Companies that Make Your Favorite Products, 272 pp. $16.95

Parenting Titles

Being a Father: Family, Work, and Self, 176 pp. $12.95

Preconception: A Woman's Guide to Preparing for Pregnancy and Parenthood, 232 pp. $14.95

Schooling at Home: Parents, Kids, and Learning, 264 pp., $14.95

Teens: A Fresh Look, 240 pp. $14.95

Automotive Titles

The Greaseless Guide to Car Care Confidence, 224 pp. $14.95

How to Keep Your Datsun/Nissan Alive, 544 pp. $21.95

How to Keep Your Subaru Alive, 480 pp. $21.95

How to Keep Your Toyota Pickup Alive, 392 pp. $21.95

How to Keep Your VW Alive, 25th Anniversary ed., 464 pp. spiral bound $25

TITLES FOR YOUNG READERS AGES 8 AND UP

American Origins Series
Each is 48 pages and $12.95 hardcover.
Tracing Our English Roots
Tracing Our French Roots
 Available 7/95
Tracing Our German Roots
Tracing Our Irish Roots
Tracing Our Italian Roots
Tracing Our Japanese Roots
Tracing Our Jewish Roots
Tracing Our Polish Roots

Bizarre & Beautiful Series
Each is 48 pages, $9.95 paperback, and $14.95 hardcover.
Bizarre & Beautiful Ears
Bizarre & Beautiful Eyes
Bizarre & Beautiful Feelers
Bizarre & Beautiful Noses
Bizarre & Beautiful Tongues

Environmental Titles
Habitats: Where the Wild Things Live, 48 pp. $9.95
The Indian Way: Learning to Communicate with Mother Earth, 114 pp. $9.95
Rads, Ergs, and Cheeseburgers: The Kids' Guide to Energy and the Environment, 108 pp. $13.95
The Kids' Environment Book: What's Awry and Why, 192 pp. $13.95

Extremely Weird Series
Each is 48 pages, $9.95 paperback, and $14.95 hardcover.
Extremely Weird Bats
Extremely Weird Birds
Extremely Weird Endangered Species
Extremely Weird Fishes
Extremely Weird Frogs
Extremely Weird Insects
Extremely Weird Mammals
Extremely Weird Micro Monsters
Extremely Weird Primates
Extremely Weird Reptiles
Extremely Weird Sea Creatures
Extremely Weird Snakes
Extremely Weird Spiders

Kidding Around Travel Series
All are 64 pages and $9.95 paperback, except for *Kidding Around Spain* and *Kidding Around the National Parks of the Southwest*, which are 108 pages and $12.95 paperback.
Kidding Around Atlanta
Kidding Around Boston, 2nd ed.
Kidding Around Chicago, 2nd ed.
Kidding Around the Hawaiian Islands
Kidding Around London
Kidding Around Los Angeles
Kidding Around the National Parks of the Southwest
Kidding Around New York City, 2nd ed.
Kidding Around Paris
Kidding Around Philadelphia
Kidding Around San Diego
Kidding Around San Francisco
Kidding Around Santa Fe
Kidding Around Seattle
Kidding Around Spain
Kidding Around Washington, D.C., 2nd ed.

Kids Explore Series
Written by kids for kids, all are $9.95 paperback.
Kids Explore America's African American Heritage, 128 pp.
Kids Explore the Gifts of Children with Special Needs, 128 pp.
Kids Explore America's Hispanic Heritage, 112 pp.
Kids Explore America's Japanese American Heritage, 144 pp.

Masters of Motion Series
Each is 48 pages and $9.95 paperback.
How to Drive an Indy Race Car
How to Fly a 747
How to Fly the Space Shuttle

Rainbow Warrior Artists Series
Each is 48 pages, $14.95 hardcover, and $9.95 paperback.
Native Artists of Africa
Native Artists of Europe
Native Artists of North America

Rough and Ready Series
Each is 48 pages, $12.95 hardcover, and $9.95 paperback.
Rough and Ready Cowboys
Rough and Ready Homesteaders
Rough and Ready Loggers
Rough and Ready Outlaws and Lawmen
Rough and Ready Prospectors
Rough and Ready Railroaders

X-ray Vision Series
Each is 48 pages and $9.95 paperback.
Looking Inside the Brain
Looking Inside Cartoon Animation
Looking Inside Caves and Caverns
Looking Inside Sports Aerodynamics
Looking Inside Sunken Treasures
Looking Inside Telescopes and the Night Sky

Ordering Information
Please check your local bookstore for our books, or call **1-800-888-7504** to order direct. All orders are shipped via UPS; see chart below to calculate your shipping charge for U.S. destinations. **No post office boxes please; we must have a street address to ensure delivery**. If the book you request is not available, we will hold your check until we can ship it. Foreign orders will be shipped surface rate unless otherwise requested; please enclose $3 for the first item and $1 for each additional item.

For U.S. Orders

Totaling	Add
Up to $15.00	$4.25
$15.01 to $45.00	$5.25
$45.01 to $75.00	$6.25
$75.01 or more	$7.25

Methods of Payment
Check, money order, American Express, MasterCard, or Visa. We cannot be responsible for cash sent through the mail. For credit card orders, include your card number, expiration date, and your signature, or call **1-800-888-7504**. American Express card orders can only be shipped to billing address of cardholder. Sorry, no C.O.D.'s. Residents of sunny New Mexico, add 6.25% tax to total.

Address all orders and inquiries to:
John Muir Publications
P.O. Box 613
Santa Fe, NM 87504
(505) 982-4078
(800) 888-7504